Lincolnshire Poppy Field

SIR JOSEPH BANKS

Rooted in Lincolnshire

by

Jean Shaftoe Burton

Jean Shaftoe

Sir Joseph Banks Society

2012

Reprinted in 2014

First published 2012 by the Sir Joseph Banks Society
Bridge Street, Horncastle, Lincolnshire LN9 5HZ
Tel: 01507 526065
Patron: Sir David Attenborough
Registered Charity No: 1127728
www.joseph-banks.org.uk

ISBN: 978-0-9572318-0-1

This volume was published with the aid of grants from:
The Lincoln Record Society and the Lincolnshire Community Foundation.

Printed in the UK by Cupit Print, Horncastle, Lincolnshire LN9 5ED

CONTENTS

Sir Joseph Banks Centre, Bridge Street, Horncastle

Acknowledgements

The publication of this book has been made possible thanks to the support of many individuals and organisations. I would like to take this opportunity to thank some of them.

I am very grateful for the grants made by the Lincoln Record Society and the Community Champions Fund managed by Lincolnshire Community Foundation, their support enabled the book to be published. I greatly appreciated the professional advice and assistance of Stuart Pearcey of Wordsman Ltd.

My sincere thanks to Neil Chambers Chief Executive of the Banks Archive Project; his support and advice has been immensely helpful. Both David Robinson OBE, Life President of the Sir Joseph Banks Society, and Neil checked the content of the book for accuracy and provided suggestions for inclusion. I greatly appreciated their contribution. The proofs were read by Judith Haddock, David Robinson, David Start and Neil Tristram and their attention to detail is much appreciated. I would, however, stress that any remaining inaccuracies or omissions are my own.

The material for this book has been collected and compiled from many sources including newspapers, magazines, local history books and exhibitions and I received help and advice from many people. I wish to offer my grateful thanks to Michael Barnsdale, Ken Blow, John Cummuck, Ian Evans, Alan James, Anthony Lodge, Simon Pawley, Mary Seaward, Michael Turland and many others who shared their knowledge with me. I also wish to acknowledge the contribution made by John R. Farnsworth's dissertation for Yale University entitled A History of Revesby 1743 - 1820.

From the beginning I hoped the book would be both interesting to the mind and attractive to the eye. To achieve the latter a group of local artists collaborated with me to create superb illustrations specifically for this publication. My grateful thanks to Douglas Addey, Olivia Branston, Mary Findell, Gwen Grantham, Sheila Grimwood, Chris Hibbins, Pat Hickson, Toni O'Neill and Delia Wakerley for their valuable contribution.

The painting of Sir Joseph Banks shown on the front cover and page 16 has been reproduced by permission of The Collection - Art and Archaeology in Lincolnshire (Usher Gallery Lincoln).

During my research I found the following publications particularly helpful:

H. C. Cameron - Sir Joseph Banks the Autocrat of the Philosophers (1952)
Harold B. Carter - Sir Joseph Banks 1743 - 1820 (1998)
J. H. Maiden - The Father of Australia (1909)

Banksias

FOREWORD

Lt. Col. John Dymoke MBE
Scrivelsby Court
Lincolnshire

'Wide as the world is, traces of you
are to be found in every corner of it'
These words, written by Robert Hobart in 1793 lie in Lincoln Cathedral,
and how very accurate they are of this great man.

I have a personal interest in Sir Joseph Banks on three counts. First, Revesby is close to my own land at Scrivelsby and one of my predecessors, Lewis Dymoke, worked with him in opening the canal from Horncastle to the River Witham in the early 1800s. Secondly, my maternal great, great grandfather, John Lindley of Royal Horticultural Society fame, as a young man worked for Banks in Soho Square. Thirdly, in 1968 I took my Battalion to Iceland for training. While there I made a courtesy call on our ambassador in Reykjavik. Who should I see on the wall behind him but a fine portrait of Sir Joseph Banks!

This book describes in detail his achievements and where he went across the globe. It is easy in the 21st century to travel by air, transmitting many millions of tons of carbon, when distant lands are a mere days journey away. Not so in the 18th century when journeys were hazardous, took months to achieve, and entailed many pitfalls.

Sir Joseph was educated at Harrow, Eton and Christ's College, Oxford, and he inherited land and a substantial income from his father. He had a large estate in Lincolnshire at Revesby, plus land in other counties. He had a significant house in Soho Square, London which eventually was to contain a vast library, reference collections, and was an international centre for research.

This book also contains résumés on the lives of Franklin, Flinders and Bass all of who were connected with Sir Joseph. Banks sailed with Cook in HMS Endeavour, and later Flinders did much to open up Australia. Many Lincolnshire names still remain around the southern coast. Nor was his interest in Australia confined to botany. He helped to establish the sheep flocks that continue to survive today. In 1779 he suggested to the House of Commons that petty criminals be transported to Australia to relieve the overcrowded English prisons. This was eventually agreed and the first ship sailed in 1786.

At the age of 40 Banks became George III's Botanical Adviser. They had a shared interest in Kew and Banks introduced Spanish Merino sheep into the Royal flock. Wool was vital to the economy in the 1700s. In 1803 Banks introduced black merino rams from Kew into the flock at Revesby (there are no black sheep there today!).

Clearly, throughout his life Banks made full use of his personal wealth for myriad enterprises and he had immense drive and verve. It is high time a book was written about his impact and influence in this county. He was a truly great product of Lincolnshire.

Lt. Col. John Dymoke MBE

INTRODUCTION

An Ongoing Journey

Life can lead us down unexpected corridors which can eventually lead to unexpected adventures. My involvement with Sir Joseph Banks is one of those fortuitous incidents. When I accepted the position of Manager at a newly opened Tourist Information Centre in Horncastle an opportunity to explore the achievements of Sir Joseph presented itself.

Mass produced information was predominant in the Centre. There was a need for a Horncastle identity and East Lindsey District Council agreed that a series of history leaflets be produced. Sir Joseph was included and by the time my research was completed I had become an ardent enthusiast.

While researching Banks's life it became obvious that he was a man of immense influence both nationally and internationally. Unlike other historic figures from Lincolnshire, Sir Isaac Newton or Sir John Franklin, his name has faded from prominence. It seemed to me the county should promote the historic link it has with this great Georgian man.

Highlighting the impact he had on the county and providing an overview of his national and international activity was an ideal foundation on which to develop his achievements. This created the theme for a book, while history trails would provide the structure onto which examples of his eclectic interests could be recorded.

The process of research and collecting information brought me into contact with many people who enjoyed discussing and sharing their Banksian experiences. This seeded the idea of forming a Sir Joseph Banks Society and it was explored as the book progressed. In the first instance it was a relatively unambitious plan but as conversations developed the project took an unexpected turn.

During an amiable discussion about the formation of a Society with a friend Jim Hopkins, we were overtaken by a wave of enthusiasm. As a result I made the wild suggestion that a Joseph Banks Centre as the Society's headquarters would be perfect. Jim's enthusiastic response was an important turning point. There was a Grade II listed building in Horncastle which was being restored by Heritage Lincolnshire. We decided to investigate the possibility of establishing it as our headquarters. The initial project of producing a book had now created its own momentum.

Having an idea is relatively easy – realising the dream is more difficult. We became a trio when Paul Scott, who was Chairman of the Horncastle Civic Trust, became involved and following discussions with the Lincolnshire Community Foundation they offered their support. In partnership with the Foundation we registered a successful bid to occupy the building. The perfect situation had been achieved, the task now was to establish a Society and secure a sustainable future for the Sir Joseph Banks Centre.

A committee of dedicated people was formed under the chairmanship of Dr. Cheryle Berry to oversee the development of the Society and Centre. Since our inauguration in 2007 we have established a Tribute Garden to Sir Joseph Banks and a book explaining how the plants are connected to Banks, a popular gift shop run by the Linkage Community Trust, commenced the establishment of a reference collection and, in partnership with East Lindsey District Council, excellent display material. New projects are already under discussion and more continue to emerge. This fascinating journey along the corridor continues and we are looking forward to an exciting future.

Jean

Jean Shaftoe Burton
Vice Chairman
Sir Joseph Banks Society

TIMELINE

Sir Joseph Banks

1743-1820

1743	Born 13th February in London
1761	Inherited Revesby estates
	Lessee of Lord of the Manor of Horncastle, Lincolnshire
1766	Expedition to Newfoundland and Labrador
	Elected Fellow of the Royal Society and Fellow of the Royal Society of Arts
	Commissioner of the Board of Longitude
1768 to 1771	Voyage with Captain James Cook to Tahiti to view Transit of Venus, New Zealand, and New Holland (now Australia)
1771	Freedom of the Borough of Boston, Lincolnshire
1772	Expedition to Hebrides and Iceland
1773	Scientific Adviser to Royal Gardens, Kew; Tour in Holland
1775	Built town house in High Street, Horncastle
1777	Acquired 32 Soho Square as London base
1778	Elected President of The Royal Society
1779	First plans for penal colony in New South Wales
1781	Created Baronet
1785	Commissioner Witham General Drainage and Navigation

1787   *Promoted transfer of breadfruit to West Indies*

       Breeding Merino sheep for transport to Australia (1809)

1788   *Treasurer of African Association*

       Founding Fellow of the Linnaean Society

1794   *Knight of the Order of the Bath*

1800   *Chaired meetings to enclose Horncastle open fields and drain East, West and Wildmore Fens, Lincolnshire*

1801   *Privy Councillor*

       Equipped Captain Matthew Flinders' circumnavigation of Terra Australis

       Financial support for mapping geology of England

1804   *Presided at foundation of Royal Horticultural Society*

1808   *Recorder of Boston*

1811   *President of the Merino Society*

1819   *Vice-President Lincolnshire Agricultural Society*

1820   *Died 19th June at Spring Grove, Heston, Middlesex*

Rosa Banksia

Sir Joseph Banks

Botanist Explorer and Patron of The Sciences

Sir Joseph Banks was pre-eminent in the world of botany and science and he maintained a wide network of contacts across the globe. He promoted Natural History within the Royal Society and initiated many practical plant projects that increased the wealth of nations. He took a particular interest in the development of Australia where his support earned him the soubriquet Father of Australia. Although his contemporaries recognised and acknowledged his status as an internationally renowned figure, history has neglected him and his name has faded from prominence.

Before success there is a beginning and an unknown future. The boy who became Sir Joseph Banks was born in Argyle Street London on the 13th February 1743, the first child of William and Sarah. Two years later, following the birth of his sister Sarah Sophia, they moved to the family home Revesby Abbey. The house, located in a small village at the edge of the Lincolnshire Fens helped to shape the future of a rich young man.

The estate had been in possession of the Banks family since 1714 when it was purchased by Sir Joseph's great grandfather. He was an articled clerk for a Sheffield lawyer and a town trustee acting as agent for the Duke of Norfolk. As his financial position improved he invested in land, and bought his first estate in Lincolnshire in 1702. Sir Joseph's grandfather continued to nurture and build on this foundation and by the time Sir Joseph's father William inherited the estate the family was well established with a secure future.

William, Sarah and their two children moved into a solid Jacobean mansion house which stood within its own parkland, surrounded by woods and copses. The gardens were designed, elms planted, a long pond dug and an orangery built and stocked. Joseph spent many happy hours wandering the fields and woods and fishing in the undrained Fens with boys from nearby villages. Perhaps it was these carefree days exploring the countryside that engendered Joseph's life long passion for the wonders of nature.

Initially he was educated at home by the Reverend Henry Shepherd, Rector of Mareham le Fen and Moorby. His formal schooling commenced at Harrow when he was nine years old, but at that time he had no real enthusiasm for the classical curriculum, preferring instead outdoor pursuits. In 1756 he was transferred to Eton as a day boy, and it was here that his interest in wild flowers and the natural world first emerged. When he went up to Christ Church Oxford in 1760 he discovered that the professor of Botany did not give lectures. Unhappy with this situation Joseph decided to pay for the services of a lecturer from Cambridge.

In 1761 Joseph's father died and two years later, on reaching his twenty-first birthday, he inherited his father's estates. This included an annual income of £6,000 and estates in Lincolnshire, Staffordshire, and Derbyshire. He now became actively involved in estate management and land drainage. With the assistance of Benjamin Stephenson, the experienced and loyal estate steward at Revesby, he expanded the work of his ancestors.

The responsibilities he acquired as a landowner did not deter his desire to expand his knowledge of the natural world. In April 1766 he joined his former school friend Lieutenant Constantine Phipps on an expedition to Newfoundland and Labrador. They sailed on HMS Niger a 32-gun frigate bound on fisheries protection under the command of Captain Thomas Adams. Banks experienced and recorded the extraordinary diversity of nature. He collected sea birds, marine life and plants from the northern seas. He also observed the inhabitants, recording their lifestyle and customs.

The return journey was marred by a severe gale during which the sea washed over the quarter deck destroying a box of seeds and plants which were destined for further study in England. His journal however survived. When he finally returned home from his first field trip abroad Banks discovered he had been appointed a Fellow of the Royal Society at the young age of twenty-three. The experience he gained during that voyage was to prove highly beneficial when two years later he embarked on what was to be the most important and challenging journey of his life.

With the support of King George III, the Royal Society approached the Admiralty to provide a vessel for a scientific journey to Tahiti to observe the passage of Venus across the disc of the sun. A Whitby collier of 368 tons was adapted as HMS Endeavour with Lieutenant James Cook in command. Banks approached the Council of the Royal Society successfully negotiating that he and his party be allowed to join the expedition. The Council wrote to the Admiralty stating:

'The Council have appointed Mr Charles Green, and Captain Cook, who is commander of the vessel, to be their observers; besides whom, Joseph Banks, Esq., Fellow of the Society, a gentleman of large fortune, who is well versed in Natural History, being desirous of undertaking the same voyage, the Council very earnestly require their Lordships, that in regard to Mr Banks's great personal merit, and for the advancement of useful knowledge, he also, together with his suite, being seven persons more (that is, eight in all) together with their baggage, be received on board of the ship in command of Captain Cook.'

The team of nine individuals were botanist Dr Daniel Solander a Swedish naturalist and friend of Banks, three young artists Sydney Parkinson, Alexander Buchan and John Reynolds, naturalist Herman Sporing and four servants, two of whom were from Revesby Peter Briscoe and James Roberts. Banks spent £10,000 providing payment for his colleagues and all necessary equipment for collecting, preserving and cataloguing material. This included a library of 100 volumes, bottles and salts for preserving specimens, nets, trawls, drags and other apparatus, and stores.

The Endeavour set sail on 25th August 1768 and she carried a food store that included:

'20 tons of ship's biscuits and flour, 1,200 gallons of beer, 1,600 gallons of spirits 4000 pieces of salted beef, 6000 pieces of salted pork, 1,500 pounds of sugar, suet, raisins, oatmeal, wheat, oil, vinegar, malt, 160 pounds of mustard seed, 107 bushels of pease stored in butts and 7,860 pounds of high-smelling fermented cabbage.'

The last item was included as Captain Cook believed it would help to prevent scurvy.

The ship sailed west, stopping at Madeira, Rio de Janeiro and Tierra del Fuego. It eventually arrived at Tahiti where the crew remained for three months. During their stay Banks compiled accurate vocabularies of the local language and learnt sufficient to hold conversations with the indigenous population. Following the observation of the transit of Venus, Cook opened the sealed orders given to him by the Admiralty. These instructed him to sail west and seek 'Terra Australis Incognita' the southern continent that was thought to exist. The orders stated:

'...after their observations on the transit of Venus they are to proceed under the direction of Banks, by order of the Lords of the Admiralty on further discoveries of the great Southern Continent...'

The vessel now sailed into uncharted waters. In October 1769 they sighted land that was described as:

Bottle Brush Tree

'displaying four or five ranges of hills rising one over the other, above all which was a chain of mountains of an enormous height.'

This was their first sighting of New Zealand. On land encounters with the Maoris required patience and tact. They were fearless and refused to be intimidated by the crew and their guns. Cook records in his log that Banks was the only crew member who learned sufficient language to communicate with Tahitians and Maoris.

To avoid confrontation with Maoris Cook decided to curtail inland exploration. He circumnavigated the two islands making detailed charts of the coast and providing names for geographic features, for example Poverty Bay, Cape Kidnappers, Cook Strait, Banks Peninsula and Cape Farewell. Cook had proved that New Zealand was not part of an undiscovered continent. Meanwhile Banks and his colleagues collected and catalogued examples of as many plants and animals as could be found on their forays on shore.

They spent six months exploring New Zealand before sailing west north west. Six months later on 28th April 1770 they found a sheltered anchorage in a bay on the east coast of New Holland (Australia). Cook named it Botany Bay as a tribute to the work of Banks and his team. While on shore many new species of plants were discovered, one of which is now called Banksia.

HMS Endeavour then sailed northwards along the east coast where they encountered the Great Barrier Reef. The ship ran onto the coral and almost foundered after it sprang a leak. They put into an estuary for repairs which necessitated their longest stop while on the East Coast. Cook named the place Endeavour River and he also claimed the area in the name of the King. It later became New South Wales.

Eucalyptus

Throughout the voyage Joseph kept a daily journal which recorded his personal view of what he saw and did. While exploring Australia he made the following entries and they are reproduced as he wrote them.

An extract from the entry for 29th May 1770 while at Thirsty Sound:

'Insects in general were plentifull, Butterflies especialy: ...the air was for the space of 3 or 4 acres crowded with them to a wonderfull degree: you could not be turned in any direction without seeing millions and yet every branch and twig was almost coverd with those that sat still: of these we took as many as we chose, knocking them down with our caps or any thing that came to hand.'

25th June he recorded the first sighting of a kangaroo:

'In gathering plants today I myself had the good fortune to see the beast so much talkd of, tho but imperfectly; he was not only like a grey hound in size and running but had a long tail, as long as grey hounds; what to liken him to I could not tell, nothing certainly that I have seen at all resembles him.'

On 12th July he wrote a detailed account of a meeting with aborigines:

'They are a very small people or at least this tribe is... Their colour was nearest to that of chocolate, not that skins were so dark but the smoak (smoke) and dirt with which they were all casd over, which I suppose servd them instead of Cloths, made them of that colour. Their hair was strait in some and curld in other, they always wore it cropped close round their heads...their eyes were in many lively and their teeth even and good;... They were all of them clean limn'd, active and nimble. Cloaths they had none, not the least rag, those parts which nature willingly conceals being exposd to view completely uncoverd; yet when they stood still they would almost always with their hand or something they held in it hide them in some measure at least, ...'

The return journey was difficult. Many of the crew suffered a malarial fever upon reaching the port at Batavia now Jakarta. At one stage only twenty men were fit enough to run the ship and twenty three died before they reached the Cape of Good Hope. Of Banks's party his two negro servants Richmond and Dorlton died of cold in Tierra del Fuego, Buckam of epilepsy in Tahiti and Parkinson, Reynold and Sporing died of the fever contracted at Batavia.

Grevillea Banksii

The three year voyage came to an end when the ship finally returned to England on the 12th June 1771. With the assistance of his colleagues Banks had amassed a huge collection of fascinating material new to science.

Banks established himself at his London home, 14 New Burlington Street and commenced the task of arranging the collections. In December 1772 the Reverend John Shepherd wrote a letter to the naturalist Gilbert White indicating the scope of the collection:

The armoury was given over to warlike instruments, mechanical instruments and utensils of every kind made by Indians in the South Seas. The second room had various native costumes

'...together with the raw material from which they were produced, as well as a large collection of insects and a complete hortus siccus of all the plants collected during the course of the voyage. The number of plants is about 3,000, 110 of which were new genera, and 1,300 new species which were never seen or heard of in Europe before.'

'The third room contained an almost numberless collection of animals, quadrupeds, birds, fish, amphibia, reptiles, insects and vermes preserved in spirits and most of them new... Add to these the choicest collection of drawings coloured by Parkinson, and 1,300 or 1,400 more drawn with each of them a flower, leaf and a portion of the stalk, coloured by the same hand.'

One of the projects Banks undertook was the cataloguing of the collection and with the assistance of Daniel Solander as botanical curator and librarian work commenced. He also employed illustrators to complete the artwork of Sydney Parkinson and paid £7,000 for nineteen master engravers to produce 743 copper plates of those drawings for a Florilegium. By 1784 the work was virtually complete.

The project had taken much longer than anticipated and the pressure to publish was waning as more explorers visited Australia and New Zealand and published details of the new species Banks had collected. This combined with spiralling costs resulted in Banks deciding to abandon publication. Eventually the illustrations and plates were left to the British Museum and later transferred to the Natural History Museum London.

After languishing for nearly 200 years the copper plates were finally brought to life in 1982. A joint venture between the museum and a specialist publisher resulted in the publication of the Banks Florilegium. Only 100 volumes were produced but they are a tribute to the skill of the young artist Sydney Parkinson who died during the voyage on HMS Endeavour.

Having withdrawn from Cook's second voyage Banks third expedition was to Iceland in 1772. Accompanied by Solander and Banks's servant from Revesby, James Roberts, they observed the geology of the country, active geysers and volcanoes. Apart from travels in Britain and Holland it was his last major voyage. He settled into a life absorbed with supporting and expanding Britain's international trade and encouraging scientific advancement.

Banks successfully established himself in English society but his voyage on HMS Endeavour continued to exert an influence on his life. In giving evidence to a House of Commons committee in 1779 he suggested that convicts be transported to Australia to relieve the chronic overcrowding of prisons in England. In 1786 the government finally agreed and the first ships sailed in May 1787 under the command of Captain Arthur Phillip. On board there were 564 men and 192 women. They landed at Botany Bay in January 1788 and on arrival Phillip became the colony's first Governor.

Before embarking on the journey Phillip submitted requests for increased food supplies, medical supplies and equipment, clothing and tools but to no avail. When the fleet landed provisions proved inadequate. Dysentery, scurvy and malnutrition became rife and many convicts died. Among official dispatches seeking advice and support from the government were long informal letters from Phillip to Banks. Sir Joseph was Australia's unofficial representative in London and he used his status and influence to obtain assistance for the struggling colony. His unstinting support earned him the title 'Father of Australia' where he continues to be an important historic figure.

His patronage and advice to explorers, governors and settlers in the colonies helped to increase Britain's wealth and influence. In 1788 Sir Joseph successfully discussed with the Directors of the East India Company the anticipated benefits of planting high yield black tea bushes from China in India. An extract from his report states why he believed this tea would help supply demand from countries like England:

'...all undertakings of new manufacture should commence with articles of inferior quality, they being less difficult in preparation and more certain (as they fall into the hands of lower people) of being admitted into immediate use than higher priced commodities, intended for consumption of those who have more distinguishing palates and fewer reasons for being economical in their purchases...'

Rosa Banksia

Shortly after returning from the Endeavour voyage Banks had been received by King George III. They respected each other's qualities and formed a long-standing friendship. As a result in 1780 Banks became involved with developments at Kew Gardens. With the King as Patron and Banks as unofficial director, the Royal Gardens were developed as a systematic botanical collection. A year later Banks spent the summer laying the foundation of Flora Kewensis, a catalogue of all the plants at Kew. Eight years later it was published and listed 5,600 species.

Kew remained a lifelong interest. It was not only a fascinating ornamental garden of exotic plants, it was also an essential tool in understanding, preserving, growing and acclimatising as many different species as could be found. He conceived the idea of making Kew a depository of every known plant that could be of use either practically or ornamentally. It was here that plants and seeds collected by Banks's network of contacts were nurtured and studied. He planted 800 species of trees and shrubs, mostly from North America, in 1773 and some still survive.

Kew trained young men to become gardeners specialising in the nurture of new species. Those with a good aptitude and the desire to travel were recruited as collectors on Royal Navy ships. When voyages of discovery were organised Banks ensured those men were on board, and as a result Kew became the foremost botanical garden in the world. During the period of his involvement 7,000 new exotic plants arrived from countries such as South Africa, India, Abyssinia and China.

To increase the survival rate of plants Sir Joseph supported the development of a glazed cabin. These were placed on the decks of ships enabling specimens from far-flung places to be successfully transported. He also participated in the development of plant experimentation helping to create the foundation on which modern horticulture is based.

He was particularly interested in economic botany, and Kew distributed plants and seeds to other botanic institutions and enterprising gardeners. In 1990 Kew named their Economic Botany Building after Sir Joseph Banks, honouring the very significant contribution he made to this branch of science.

Joseph was influential in the exploration of the continent of Africa. During the return journey of HMS Endeavour, Banks and Solander spent a few days on shore at the Cape of Good Hope observing the local flora and fauna. It was sufficient time for them to recognise the potential for trade and the advancement of botany.

Banks helped organise Francis Masson's trip to the Cape of Good Hope to collect specimens for Kew. When he returned to England three years later Masson had amassed a large collection of plants. The success of this expedition resulted in Masson travelling to South Africa on three further occasions as well as spending time in Portugal, the West Indies and finally Canada where he died. He spent his life in the service of Kew where his name is still honoured.

Sir Joseph was also instrumental in founding the African Association on 7th June 1788 when an informal group of like-minded people came together to promote the exploration of inland Africa. In 1795 the Association sponsored Mungo Park's famous explorations of the River Niger. The association disbanded in 1831 the same year that the Royal Geographical Society was established.

Sir Joseph actively encouraged and supported organisations and individuals interested in expanding their knowledge of the natural world. He was a founding member of what is now the Royal Horticultural Society. On 14th March 1804 the first meeting took place at Mr. Hatchard's of Piccadilly, with Sir Joseph in the chair.

When Swedish botanist Carl Linnaeus died his heirs offered Sir Joseph his massive collection of herbarium, zoological and mineral samples together with his library and correspondence. Instead of accepting Banks encouraged medical student James Edward Smith to undertake the purchase and organisation of the collections. When the Linnaean Society was inaugurated in 1788 Banks was one of only three honorary Fellows elected.

George III had great respect for Banks's ability and knowledge in the world of botany and agriculture. In particular they had a shared interest in wool production which played a major role in England's economy in the 18th century. Although the official figure for sheep in England was over 25 million the country still had to import fine wool from Spain. To improve wool production Banks initiated the introduction of Spanish Merino sheep into the Royal flock in 1787. During a period of political tension Banks managed to organise the shipping of 300 sheep from Spain. Integration however proved difficult and it took ten years to establish sizeable flocks at which point Banks was able to relinquish responsibility for the project.

During the winter of 1803 Banks introduced pure black Merino rams from Kew into the flock at Revesby. From this flock Captain John Macarthur, a leading sheep farmer in New South Wales, purchased six shearling rams. In 1805 he transported them to Australia to improve the breeding stock there.

In 1777 Banks decided to move house and purchased 32 Soho Square as his permanent London address. Two years later he married Dorothea Hugessen, an heiress from Kent, and they set up home there with Banks's sister Sarah Sophia. As Sir Joseph's reputation continued to grow his London home became a focal point for visiting scientist from across the world.

Every morning, when in residence, the library, reception rooms and the herbarium were open to visitors. On tables he laid the latest works on scientific subjects for guests to peruse and discuss. Fires burned brightly and tea, coffee and rolls were served. Once a week he invited guests to a formal reception where a pre-selected subject would be debated.

His dedication to science was recognised when he was elected to become a member of the Council of the Royal Society in 1774, then President in 1778, a position he held until his death forty-two years later. During his association with the Royal Society he attended 417 out of 450 meetings

Violet

and handled at least 50,000 items of correspondence. Sir Joseph considered his Presidency the most important and prestigious of the many honours bestowed on him. These included a Baronetcy in 1781 and on 22nd March Banks received the following instruction:

'...I am directed by Lord North to acquaint You His Majesty has been graciously pleased to sign a Warrant for creating You a Baronet of Great Britain, and that You may kiss Hands at the Levee Tomorrow.'

The next day Banks attended at the Court of St. James and left as Baronet of Revesby in the County of Lincolnshire.

In 1794 he received the Order of the Bath, became a Privy Councillor in 1801, and had honorary memberships to learned societies both in this country and abroad. Banks was thus in a position to influence and support experimental work in all the sciences and many scientists received his patronage.

Lapwing

An example of this support was his involvement in land measurement. In 1784 he worked with General William Roy, director of military surveys, as they strove to accurately measure a five mile stretch of land on Hounslow Heath. Initially chains were used but these expanded and contracted as the temperature fluctuated. Then wooden poles were tried but they were affected by humidity. Finally special glass tubes were successfully utilised.

The project took all summer provoking great interest and many visitors, including the King. This formed part of a larger experiment to measure the distance between the Royal Observatories of Greenwich and Paris in 1787. The Hounslow Heath baseline was the first step in the development of the Ordnance Survey we know today. When in the 19th century it was reassessed an error of only two inches along its full length was recorded.

During his Presidency of the Royal Society Banks was involved in the publication of more than a thousand papers representing all branches of science. His knowledge in the field of botany was highly respected and his contacts radiated across the globe. He corresponded with foreign governments offering advice on how best to promote their natural resources. It was he who organised the shipping of mangoes to Jamaica and masterminded the scheme to transport breadfruit from the Pacific to the West Indies on HMS Bounty under the command of Captain William Bligh.

Canada Geese

Although his activities in London were demanding Sir Joseph still maintained very close links with his childhood home, Revesby Abbey. He owned 268 tenanted farms in Lincolnshire and thousands of acres of land. The estates farmed crops, woods for coppicing, sheep for wool and meat, deer for venison as well as other livestock.

Meadowsweet

Arthur Young, the Secretary of the Board of Agriculture and friend of Sir Joseph wrote an excellent description in 1799 of how efficiently Banks organised his office at Revesby:

'...His office, of two rooms, is contained in the space of thirty feet by sixteen; there is a brick partition between, with an iron plated door, so that the room in which a fire is always burning might be burnt down without affecting the inner one, where he has 150 drawers... the inside being thirteen inches wide by eight broad, and five and a half deep, all numbered. There is a catalogue of names and subjects, and a list of every paper in every drawer, so that whether the inquiry concerns a man, or a drainage, or an enclosure, or a farm, or a weed, the request was scarcely named before a mass of information was in a moment before me. Fixed tables are before the windows (to the south), on which are spread maps, plans etc., commodiously, and these labelled, are arranged against the wall. The first room contains desks, tables, and bookcase, with measures, levels etc and a wooden case which when open forms a bookcase, and joining in the centre by hinges. When closed forms a package ready for a carrier's wagon, containing forty folio paper-cases in the form of books; a repository of such papers as are wanted equally in town and country. Such an apartment, and such an apparatus, must be of incomparable use in the management of any great estate; or, indeed, of any considerable business.'

Sir Joseph's status ensured he was a man of influence in his home county. He was High Sheriff of Lincolnshire in 1794 and Lt. Col. Supplemental Militia Northern Battalion Lincolnshire in 1797. He was also proactive in the draining of East, West and Wildmore Fens and the development of canals in the county. He supported and sponsored Lincolnshire explorers Matthew Flinders and George Bass. When he returned to the county each autumn he become actively involved in the management of his estates and chaired many boards and committees in Lincolnshire. While in residency he also organised annual social events such as the Fishing Party on the River Witham – he recorded a description of one such outing:

'We drew ten miles of fresh water, and in four days caught seventeen hundredweight of fish; dining from twenty to thirty masters and mistresses with servants and

Yellow Iris

attendants, of the fish we had caught, dressed at fires on the banks; and when we were done we had not 10lbs of fish left.'

In addition there was the Revesby Fair, Lincoln Races, the Stuff Ball at Lincoln and the Dispensary Ball at Horncastle all important dates in the county's social calendar.

Sir Joseph had a significant impact on Lincolnshire's economic status. He promoted wool production and forestry. He was involved in the development of canals improving the county's transport infrastructure. He was also involved in drainage and enclosure of Fens transforming marsh and bog into fertile agricultural land increasing food production. His direct involvement in the county continued until ill health prevented his annual visits, and thereafter he relied heavily on correspondence with his steward at Revesby.

Sir Joseph died in 1820 at his residence at Spring Grove in Middlesex, and was buried in St Leonard's Church Heston marked only by a plain stone. In his Will he acknowledged the loyal service he had received from friends and employees. Two beneficiaries were his friend and librarian Robert Brown, who received an annuity of £200 a year together with his library and herbarium, and Francis Bauer, an artist who had served him for thirty years received an annuity of £300. In his Will he stated:

'I entreat my dear relatives to spare themselves the affliction of attending the ceremony and I earnestly request that they will not erect any monument to my memory.'

An inevitable result of this request was that fifty years after his death the position of his grave was in danger of being lost.

In 1867 Dr Gray, Keeper of the Zoological Department of the British Museum wrote to the Revd. E. Spooner enquiring about the location of his grave. The vicar replied that a vault had been opened during rebuilding work and a coffin was discovered bearing his name. He further explained that he had arranged for a marble tablet to be erected in the church with the inscription:

'In this church is buried the Right Honourable Sir Joseph Banks BART, KB, President of the Royal Society 1778-1820. Died at Spring Grove 19th June 1820. Aged 77.'

Shortly after Banks's death a close friend, Charles Hatchett, commented:

He 'never pretended to be deeply versed in any branch of science, he possessed, nonetheless, no small share of scientific knowledge and was a living index of facts, especially pertaining to the skills and knowledge of others.'

The role Sir Joseph accepted was that of facilitator and it left him little time to publish or promote himself as an unrivalled expert in any particular branch of science. Harold Carter Banks's biographer wrote:

'there is scarcely an aspect of British public life in the reign of George III which is not represented at first hand by the correspondence of Sir Joseph Banks.'

His written legacy is his correspondence. It is estimated that he received and sent around 50,000 letters during his lifetime. These covered many aspects of life and spanned every corner of the world. He wished to further the interest of science and he achieved this by bringing key people together, financing projects, sponsoring individuals and ensuring good communications with scientists across the globe regardless of political issues. Banks once commented:

'It has, indeed, been always my wish to promote the scientific intercourse among nations, notwithstanding any political divisions which might subsist between them.'

Sir Joseph's impact on the world is incalculable. Through his involvement with commercial enterprises and interaction with foreign governments he influenced the future of continents, as demonstrated by the soubriquet 'Father of Australia'. He was instrumental in altering attitudes towards nature and agriculture. He initiated and promoted research into new techniques and ideas, and encouraged scientific exploration. He was a true patron of the sciences and generously supported scientific projects. He spent his life acquiring and sharing knowledge. There can be few men who achieved such a lasting effect on the world. The tribute to Sir Joseph in Lincoln Cathedral has the words:

'Wide as the world is, traces of you are to be found in every corner of it.' (Robert Hobart 1793)

a simple accolade that acknowledges Sir Joseph's immense contribution to development across the globe.

Trail Route Planner

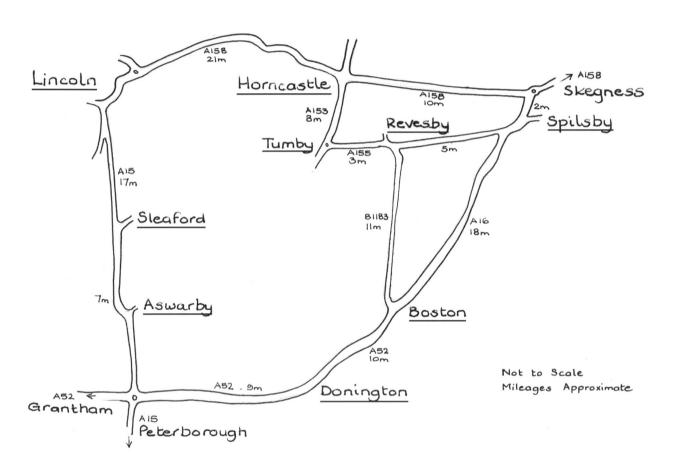

JOSEPH BANKS COUNTRY
Revesby

Lych Gate

Revesby is situated five miles to the south east of Horncastle and was rebuilt in the mid-nineteenth century. Today it is a charming village with cottages and almshouses in a horseshoe shape round a beautifully kept village green.

The original village was recorded in the Domesday survey of 1086 and in 1142 the first Earl of Lincoln gave the land to the monks of Rievaulx to establish a monastery. Following dissolution of the monasteries Henry VIII gave the estate to the Duke of Suffolk. Its ownership passed through other hands before being acquired by Sir Joseph Banks's great grandfather in 1714. Joseph inherited Revesby Estate on the death of his father William in 1761.

Joseph spent his early childhood roaming the estate. He was educated at home until he was nine when he was sent to Harrow, and then Eton and finally going up to Oxford where he read natural sciences. Following his marriage to Dorothea Hugessen in 1779 he visited Revesby virtually every year up to 1817. He dealt with estate matters and attended social events. In early October there was the Revesby Fair. The servants' hall was thrown open, booths appeared in the village and Sir Joseph provided beef, bread and ale for estate workers and visitors.

He owned 9,383 enclosed acres providing a livelihood for 400 tenants and contributing a gross income of some £5,500. Banks was considered a benevolent landlord and on the rare occasion when a farm became vacant (he preferred to pass farms to the tenant's heir) there were many applications for tenure. He was highly respected and held important public positions including Recorder of Boston and High Sheriff of Lincolnshire.

Although Sir Joseph owned other estates and lived most of the year in London, he always regarded Revesby as his home. During Flinders' circumnavigation of Australia he named an island Revesby highlighting the link the continent has with Banks and Lincolnshire.

Revesby Village Trail

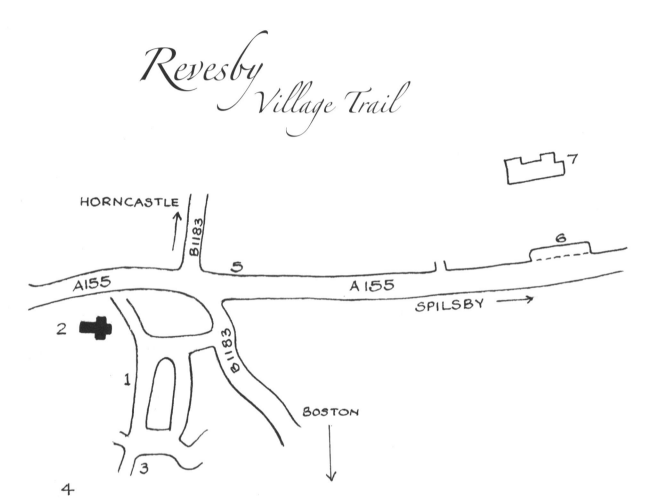

1. Almshouses

As instructed in Sir Joseph's great grandfather's Will The Almshouses were built in 1729 on Revesby Green for 'ten decayed agriculturists' or their widows over sixty. The residents also received an income of £5 a year. These houses were built of brick and thatch at a cost of £350.

The houses were rebuilt in 1862 by James Banks Stanhope who inherited the estate on the death of Dorothea Banks in 1828. The houses were restored and modernised in 1987 to provide five homes for people of retirement age. There is an explanatory plaque on the wall.

Almshouse

2. The Church of St. Lawrence

The church was built by James Banks Stanhope and his nephew Edward in 1891 replacing the earlier church of 1730. The lych-gate commemorates the death of the Rt. Hon. Edward Stanhope, Secretary of State for War who died 1893.

i. There is a model of the earlier Georgian church near the font.

ii. In the main vestry are panels from the Georgian church and a coloured print of the demolished Revesby Abbey home of Sir Joseph. The sanctuary floor tiles are copies of the medieval tiling from the monastery church.

iii. On the west wall of the north aisle there is a monument to the Banks family. The banner above the monument was commissioned when Sir Joseph was awarded the Order of the Bath, one of many honours bestowed on him during his life. Sir Joseph's coat of arms is also in this corner of the church.

iv. In the sanctuary on the south wall there is a plaque in memory of Richard Stanhope, who was Squire of Revesby until his death during World War I. The stained glass windows on both sides are also in his memory. The east window and a plaque on the north wall are dedicated to Edward and James Banks Stanhope.

(There are leaflets in the church providing more detailed information about its history).

In the churchyard near the porch, there is a marble obelisk (the Latin inscription has unfortunately worn away) dedicated to the memory of the first Joseph Banks who gave the estate much of its basic character. The sarcophagus and bust were removed from the original grave site and placed inside the church, but the obelisk was considered too large. It was buried in an adjacent farmyard where it remained until it was discovered in 1972.

The Old Post Office

3. Georgian House – The Old Post Office

The homes around the village green were built by the Stanhope's in the 1850s. The only building dating back to the Georgian period is a shop now converted to a house called The Old Post Office. Unfortunately during the modernisation process it lost much of its original character. However its survival is a link with the Banks dynasty and their efforts to provide improved facilities for their estate workers.

The 1881 census listed occupations including: groom, housemaid, dairy maid, master blacksmith, master joiner, shepherd, wagoner, dress maker, laundress, servants and labourers.

4. Cistercian Monastery

The Abbey at Revesby was founded in 1142 on land given by the first Earl of Lincoln. It is situated outside the main village in a field behind the village hall. The monks specialised in rearing sheep for wool and had rights on the undrained Fens. They also provided accommodation for lay brothers who did most of the farming. The Order flourished until 1539 when Henry VIII ordered the dissolution of monasteries. Sadly all that remains of the Abbey today are mounds that trace the outline of buildings. The site however is listed as an ancient monument (there is an informative leaflet in the church).

5. Red Lion Revesby

The inn was built in 1862 in similar style to the rest of the village. It is situated on the A155 with road connections to Horncastle, Spilsby and Boston and was a coaching inn. Originally it was part of Revesby estate but it is now privately owned. There is little change to the exterior but internally it has been modernised.

Red Lion Revesby

6. Revesby Abbey Gates

On the A155 in the direction of East Kirkby stand the ornamental gates leading to Revesby Abbey. The screen and gates were erected in 1848 and used to be the main entrance to the Abbey. From here the privately owned mansion can be glimpsed.

The parkland has changed little over the past 250 years. Sir Joseph released kangaroos in the park and he planted seeds and cuttings which had been sent to him from around the world. Two palm trees still survive in the arboretum. He also introduced Spanish Merinos into his flock at Revesby and six shearlings were transported to Australia helping to improve the breeding stock. During Sir Joseph's tenure the parkland provided grazing for up to twenty Scottish cattle, twenty-five to sixty sheep, a few cows for milk, six wagon horses and six saddle horses and a herd of deer.

The Estate provided a steady supply of food for Sir Joseph's London homes. A weekly hamper sent by coach from Horncastle contained in season venison, partridges, woodcock, hares, and pike. In April peewit eggs were packed in sawdust, and during the winter months he received a doe each week.

Benjamin Stephenson was steward at Revesby from 1741 - 1792 and is buried in the churchyard at Revesby. He sent weekly reports to Sir Joseph on all matters related to the Revesby Estate, tenanted farms and his business interests in Lincolnshire. He also kept him updated on social changes within the county.

Revesby Abbey Gate Pillar

7. Revesby Abbey

The home of Sir Joseph was called Revesby Abbey as its location was believed to be the site of the Abbot's house during the period the land was occupied by the Cistercian monastery.

Sir Joseph maintained a large household, one of whom was James Roberts. He was a native of Mareham le Fen where he is buried. His headstone is in the church of St Helen and it reads:

'Here lies the body of James Roberts, who in the years 1768 - 1771 sailed round the world with the Right Honourable Sir Joseph Banks on His Majesty's ship the Endeavour, Lieutenant James Cook, Commander. In the year 1772 he again made a voyage with Sir J. Banks to Iceland and ascended the summit of that wonderful burning mountain, Hecla.

Having returned in safety to England, he retired in 1795 to Mareham House and died on the 8th of July, 1826, aged 74 years.'

In October 1793 Banks received a visit from Matthew Flinders, a midshipman in the Royal Navy, who had travelled from his home in Donington. During the visit Sir Joseph reimbursed him for an advance of £30 to a gardener who had been collecting plants and seeds for Banks while Matthew was on board HMS Providence under Captain William Bligh.

The Estate hosted the annual Revesby Fair which was a popular pleasure fair. Revesby Abbey ale was drunk and a bullock was roasted. Banks noted in a letter dated 20th October 1783:

'This is the day of our fair when according to immemorial custom I am to feed and make drunk everyone who chooses to come, which will cost me in beer and ale near £20, and I am sure there is no quiet in the house all day.'

The present Revesby Abbey

Revesby Abbey

The present Revesby Abbey was built in 1844 for James Banks Stanhope. The architect was the Scottish born William Burn who specialised in building manor houses for the wealthy both in Scotland and England.

Burn's incorporated new concepts into his designs and was one of the first to provide a family wing as an integral part of a manor house. He promoted interconnecting formal rooms so that partitions could be closed for private use, creating smaller more comfortable rooms for the family. He was also an early proponent of corridor building enabling people to move around the house without passing through rooms. All these design features improved the privacy afforded to the occupants of important country houses.

Revesby Abbey is in the Jacobean style and the interior has beautifully decorated plaster ceilings and cornices. The panelled hallway and landing has a ceiling covered with heraldic shields depicted in glorious colours. Many of the features in this grand country house are currently in need of restoration.

Revesby Abbey is a Grade I listed building. Its historic value is considerably enhanced by the fact that the layout of rooms has not substantially altered from the original Burn's design and provides a particularly good example of his style. It is now in such a state of disrepair that it appears on the Buildings at Risk register compiled by English Heritage.

The Abbey is situated on the estate where Sir Joseph spent most his childhood and visited annually for most of his adult years. The income from the estate virtually funded all Banks's activities in collecting, science and exploration. The parkland has hardly changed from the time he released kangaroos in the grounds. The home Sir Joseph knew was demolished and stood a short distance from the present building. Although this country house is not the actual home of Sir Joseph his connection with the estate provides another important reason for ensuring its survival.

Church of St Lawrence, Revesby

JOSEPH BANKS COUNTRY
Forest Walk

The Banks Estates included Fulsby Wood, Tumby Wood, Shire Wood and Revesby Park, all of which played an important role in the financial success of the estate. There is evidence that St Helen's, part of Tumby Wood, is an ancient forest. During Banks's time the woodland management was coppice with standards to maximise its commercial value.

During the 18th and 19th centuries timber was a valuable resource and forestry was more profitable than it is today. Sir Joseph was acknowledged as the most scientific planter in Lincolnshire until he was eclipsed by the Earl of Yarborough. He practised a system of rotation and selective felling which produced high quality timber that was much sought after and commanded premium prices. His profit, nearly £2 an acre, was double that of the national average for woodland in England in the 18th century.

There are approximately 750 acres of woodland at Tumby and they made a significant contribution to the income of Revesby Estate. Following the death of Dorothea Banks in 1828 the estate was divided and the Hawley family inherited this forest.

1. St. Helen's Wood

Situated at Tumby on the A153 there is a public right of way on the edge of St Helen's Wood which is classified as ancient woodland. Follow the public path to the Lea Gate Inn. Sir Joseph would have managed it in a way that provided trees suitable for coppicing and felling.

During his visit to Lincolnshire in May 1768, just prior to sailing on HMS Endeavour, Banks increased the number of Scots pines. He harvested the seeds from mature pines, oak and birch and used them to increase coverage on his own estates and elsewhere in England. He also supplied saplings for planting at the Earl of Yarborough's estate, Brocklesby Park, and for Willingham House near Market Rasen a new mansion built for the MP of Great Grimsby.

Spruce

2. Native Trees

The wood is comprised of predominantly native species. The main tree cover is larch, Scots pine, hazel, silver birch and oak. The sycamore which is an introduced species and officially classified as a weed, is unlikely to have been part of the managed wood. Over the decades they have probably self-seeded from trees on neighbouring land. The larch was a native tree before the Ice Age and had to be reintroduced as it did not colonise our shores afterwards.

3. Forest Management

Tumby Wood had been carefully nurtured from 1727 when Sir Joseph's great grandfather managed the wood. It contained oak, willow, alder, hazel, ash and elm. Sir Joseph operated a system of rotation and selective felling so that at twenty three year intervals every acre was properly thinned.

Larch

Originally managed woods were predominantly hazel and oak. The hazel, which can be coppiced, is a small bushy tree growing beneath the standards, usually oak. Sir Joseph managed his woods so that there was a regular supply of timber which was renowned for its high quality.

The oaks were left for four or five periods of rotation (92 - 115 years) before being felled. On average around 600 were for sale each year. Hazel, alder and willow were cut after one period, ash and elm were cut if full grown after twenty-three years, but the best stood for another term. Nothing was wasted, the timber, pole pieces, bark and even the brash all found buyers.

On 26th September 1809 the estate lost 103 valuable oak trees when a hurricane swept through Lincolnshire.

Oak

Royal Oak, Mareham le Fen.
Mud and stud building

4. Commercial Markets

Hazel provided laths for the mud and stud method of building and examples can be seen in Mareham le Fen. Hazel was also used for fencing. The bark of thinned oak would be sold to the tanning trade another activity operating during Sir Joseph's lifetime. Larch and Scots pine provided straight lengths suitable for poles and fencing. In 1797 Sir Joseph's estate manager, John Parkinson, calculated that the woodland yielded an income of just under £2 per acre per annum.

Each autumn the steward, bailiff and woodkeeper laid out and valued the lots to be sold by auction that winter, then marked the trees for identification. Printed advertisements appeared giving the auction dates for each wood. For Revesby the auction took place at the Red Lion in Revesby and for Tumby at The Swan (now a private house) on the A153 in the direction of Coningsby. Before the sales prospective purchasers inspected the trees and once bought they were marked and left standing until the following spring. At that time the sap would be rising and the bark could be peeled more easily.

White Swan

5. Trees Lining Path

In the agricultural system of today woods do not command the commercial value they once did and as a result they are not managed with the same care or intensity. Although this wood contains elements of Sir Joseph's management, the forest cover has changed over the centuries. Silver birch is abundant on the fringes of the path and there are clusters of oak, some about 100 years old. The larch with its weeping boughs is a dominant species with the Scots pine and spruce intermingling.

Stump Puffball

At various times of year you will see a profusion of wild flowers, ferns, fungi, bramble bushes and, of course, the less popular stinging nettle.

6. First World War

During the First World War there was a heavy demand for timber and as a result many woods were depleted. In an effort to redress the situation the Forestry Commission was established in 1919 to co-ordinate regeneration, and they still manage large tracts of woodland throughout the country. St Helens is a privately owned wood.

Bramble

7. Second World War

There is a crater near the fence separating the wood from the field path leading to the Lea Gate Inn, probably created by a bomb. During the Second World War planes would discharge unused bombs before landing at RAF Coningsby. It was common practice to dump them in woods and forest to contain blast damage.

8. *Lea Gate Inn*

You could start or finish your walk at this popular old inn situated at one of the 'gates' to Wildmore Fen. The Lea Gate was built in the mid 16th century as a 'guide house and hostelry'. It appears on a manuscript map dated 1560 which would suggest that it was a licensed house from that date. It was also known as Leeds Gate and the track south through Wildmore Fen led to a ferry crossing the Witham at Langrick.

The Lea Gate offered a place of respite providing warmth and comfort for weary travellers. Here they would wait until a guide who was familiar with the terrain came to escort them across the hazardous Fen to a destination of safety.

Lea Gate Inn

Tinkers

JOSEPH BANKS COUNTRY
Horncastle

St Mary's Square

Horncastle is the nearest market town to Revesby and during the 18th and 19th centuries it was a bustling commercial centre. It provided essential services and facilities for the surrounding villages and acted as a distribution point for produce and raw materials. During this period Sir Joseph played a leading role in the construction of the Horncastle canal providing a link via the River Witham with the international port at Boston and the city of Lincoln.

In addition to Revesby Estate the Banks family leased the Manor of Horncastle from the Bishop of Carlisle who had held it since 1230. Sir Joseph and his steward became involved with rights, tolls, markets and property management. He also helped provide facilities for the community such as the school and dispensary. During his visits he also attended a number of important social events one being the annual Dispensary Ball at the Bull Hotel.

During Sir Joseph's life Horncastle was famous for its August Horse Fair which later in the 19th century became the largest in the world. This annual event ceased in the 1940s. The open market continues on Thursdays and Saturdays, although the town is now best known for its antique shops. There have been many changes over the centuries but Banks's impact still survives.

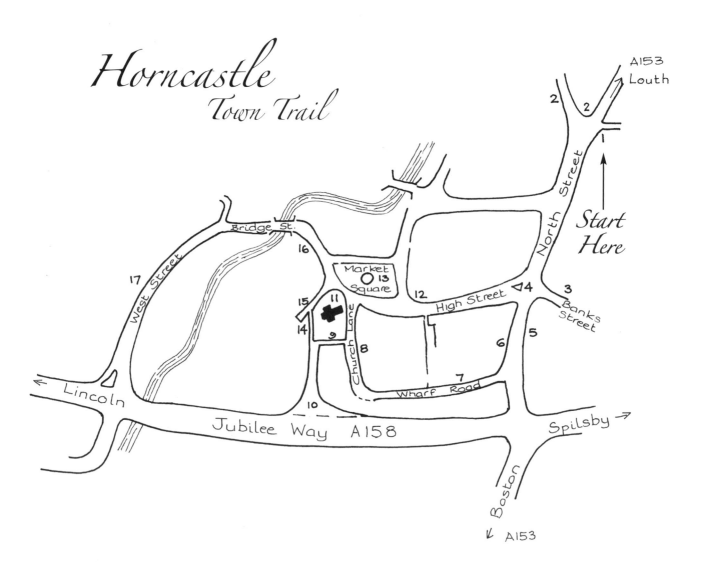

Horncastle
Town Trail

1. *War Memorial Hospital* - North Street

On the death of the King's Champion Sir Henry Dymoke in 1865 (the ceremonial title is still held by the Dymoke family who live at Scrivelsby) the community decided to erect a new dispensary in North Street. This tribute acknowledged Sir Henry's unfailing support for the earlier Dispensary founded by Dr Edward Harrison and supported by Sir Joseph Banks. This building was completed in 1866 and cost £1,026 10s. 11d to construct and furnish. It was supported by subscriptions and legacies and continued to assist members of the community who were unable to afford medical care.

Following the First World War Horncastle's tribute to their war heroes was to extend the dispensary to provide cottage hospital facilities. £2,200 was raised by public subscription and in June 1924 it was officially opened. It provided beds for seven patients together with an operating theatre, bathroom and kitchens.

The hospital closed in March 1998 and now provides a variety of services for the community.

2. *The Angel Inn and Tax Office* - North Street

The large building opposite the former hospital was the Court House built in 1865. Prior to that the parish stocks stood there. It has now been converted into offices. The Oddfellows, a benevolent society established in the Victorian era, once had an interest in the Angel Inn. A pub has stood on this site since 1720.

3. *Banks Street*

This road was named in honour of Sir Joseph Banks and on the south side there is a terrace of well-preserved Georgian houses.

Pub sign

Banks Street

The Bull Ring

4. *The Bull Ring*

The Bull Ring was the location of the Beast Market where livestock were sold.

Sir Joseph moved this market to the Wong in 1792 and the Vestry had the area paved. Sir Joseph levied a toll of one pence per head of cattle sold, and two pence for all horses put up for sale at these markets. The Bull Ring was also the centre of the Great August Horse Fair.

5. *The Bull Hotel - The Bull Ring*

Although the frontage is 19th century there are buildings at the rear dating from the 16th century. Originally it was a coaching inn and provided stabling. In the rear yard the original cobbling still exists. The inn was often used for business meetings.

Banks chaired one such meeting in 1799 when John Rennie was asked to conduct a survey of the East, West and Wildmore Fens and provide proposals for draining them. The committee resolved:

'that the thanks of the meeting be given to the Chairman for his unremitting care and attention in promoting this most beneficial work.'

The report was submitted in 1800 followed by meetings at Horncastle and Boston with landowners some of whom had forceful objections. Despite this the necessary Acts of Parliament were passed in 1801, 1802 and 1803 and Commissioners were appointed to carry out the work.

The Bull Hotel was also the venue for the annual Dispensary Ball attended by Sir Joseph and Lady Banks. It was considered one of the most fashionable events in Lincolnshire. The Ball was held in the Assembly Room which was part of the taller building on the right of the main hotel. It is the room behind the large first floor window.

6. King's Head - The Bull Ring

It is the only thatched inn in Horncastle, and is known locally as *The Thatch*. It is one of the few remaining mud and stud buildings in the town and dates from the 16th century.

The King's Head

7. Wharf Road

In 1791 Sir Joseph chaired a meeting at the Bull Hotel when it was decided a canal should be constructed to provide a link to the River Witham and the international port at Boston. Banks persuaded landowners to finance the project which would develop and improve the existing Tattershall canal. In 1793 the venture commenced but the funds proved insufficient to complete the project. Work ceased until Banks and Lord Fortescue each loaned the Navigation Company £10,000. Banks was elected President of the Horncastle Navigation and served for twenty-seven years.

The canal was eleven miles long and had a fall of eighty-four feet. It required a new cut from Horncastle to Dalderby and the River Bain was deepened and straightened allowing fifty ton vessels to reach the wharf. There were twelve locks and the work was completed at a cost of £45,000 four times the original estimate. On 17th September 1802 a public holiday was called to celebrate the opening of the canal. Two thousand spectators cheered and a band played rousing tunes as three vessels were pulled into the basin.

The quayside became a very active area. Barges transported coal, grain and wool while packet boats carried passengers from Lincoln and Boston. Many new businesses flourished and there were warehouses and offices leading into narrow alleyways like Tinkers Entry (now named Lindsey Court). These provided access to the Market Place. The railway arrived in 1855 and gradually replaced the need for the canal. Trade declined until finally in 1878 the canal ceased to operate.

Tinkers Entry

8. Marwood's Shop - Church Lane

In Church Lane opposite the church there is a small building on which a blue plaque has been placed. It was here that William Marwood continued his trade as a cobbler following his appointment as one of England's executioners in 1872. He kept a large stock of shoe laces which were sold to sightseers who visited the shop in the hope of meeting him.

9. The Original Dispensary and Workhouse

At the south side of the churchyard there is a white house with a blue plaque that acknowledges it as being The Dispensary (1789 - 1866). Annual outbreaks of smallpox greatly concerned Sir Joseph and he called a public meeting at the Bull Hotel on 28th October 1789 to discuss the situation. Those present appointed him the first President of The Dispensary which was one of the earliest in England. In its first year the Dispensary treated 9,253 patients. In 1790 when another outbreak of smallpox occurred inoculations were offered free to those who could not afford them. It was relocated in 1866 to what was to become the War Memorial Hospital.

The Dispensary and Workhouse

Dr Edward Harrison was appointed Physician in 1790 a position he held for 31 years. Patients from as far away as Boston, Grantham and Lincoln came for diagnosis and medication. Some medicines were acquired in London by Sir Joseph. The Annual General Meeting was convened to coincide with his annual visits to Revesby. The Dispensary was supported by subscriptions, donations and the Annual Ball held at the Bull Hotel.

In October 1804 Dorothea refers to the Ball in a letter sent to a friend in Northamptonshire:

'Next Thursday we are to go to Horncastle, a neighbouring town, where an Annual Sermon is to be preached for the benefit of a Dispensary, of which Sir Joseph is President, and, by way of encouraging people to come and subscribe, there is to be a dance. We shall make our appearance but not stay late, and come home again, and it's a very good road.'

Another blue plaque on the neighbouring building denotes the workhouse which operated at the premises from 1735 - 1837. It was built by public subscription and remained in use until the Union Workhouse was established at the edge of town.

10. St Mary's Square

This is a delightful passageway leading from the church to the former canal and town centre bypass. It contains two thatched cottages and a house reputed to have been owned by William Marwood Executioner for England from 1872- 1883. He was famous for developing the Long Drop, a method of hanging that ensured instant death.

11. Church of St Mary

In 1153 it is recorded that a vicar was appointed to St. Mary's suggesting a church existed at that time. The oldest part of the present building is the west tower which dates back to the 12th-13th century. Most of the green Spilsby sandstone came from the Roman Walls that once existed in the town. The stone was quarried at Holbeck near Tetford. When Sir Joseph held the Manor the church had boxed pews and it was neglected with windows bricked up and crumbling walls.

On 10th September 1859 a public meeting was held and James Banks Stanhope who was a Lay Reader at St. Mary's presided. Major restoration work was undertaken in 1861 and Banks Stanhope bore the expense of repairing the chancel.

12. Banks's Town House - High Street

Fronting the High Street at the corner of the Market Place is a building Sir Joseph commissioned as his Town House in 1775. This enabled him to attend to his town commitments as Lindsey magistrate as well as attending meetings to discuss the Horncastle Canal, enclosure of the town's open fields and proposals to drain and enclose the East, West and Wildmore Fens.

Banks's Town House

There is a blue plaque on the wall. The ground floor houses shops which were established after his death in 1820 however the upper floor remains virtually as it was during Sir Joseph's life.

13. *Stanhope Memorial* - *Market Place*

The monument in the centre of the Market Place was erected in 1899. The memorial acknowledges the contribution made to Horncastle and its residents by the Rt. Hon. Edward Stanhope who was MP for the Horncastle Division from 1874 - 1893. Stanhope was a generous benefactor to the town donating money and land.

During Sir Joseph's life the space was occupied by houses, shops and warehouses. When Edward Stanhope held the Manor of Horncastle he relinquished the market tolls and rents to the Town Council on the undertaking that they demolish the buildings and re-establish the former open market place. Edward Stanhope was at the forefront of many welfare improvements and it is claimed he died from overwork.

Stanhope Memorial

14. *National School* - *Manor House Street*

In 1814 the National School was built. Sir Joseph gave the land free of rent and donated some 200 trees including 24 ash, 5 elms, 1 maple and 1 beech from his Revesby Estate. The unused timber was sold by auction realising a further £64 15s for funds. He also made a donation of £94 15s. and provided an annual subscription of £10.

The school had one master at an annual salary of £80 who delegated teaching duties to monitors chosen from among the pupils. By this method the school supervised and instructed 251 pupils. The school building has undergone alterations since its inception and is now a Community Centre.

15. *The Manor House* - *Manor House Street*

The Manor House

Opposite the school, behind a high brick wall with a blue plaque, stands the Manor House once owned by the Bishop of Carlisle. Dr Charles Lyttleton was a sponsor for Sir Joseph at his election as Fellow of the Royal Society in April 1766. Banks made his first appearance at the Society on 15th February 1767 following his return from a voyage to Newfoundland and Labrador. Dr Lyttleton was also President of the Society of Antiquaries and Banks became a fellow in 1766.

Beyond the Manor House is Banovallum House built on Banks estate land. It is the headquarters of the Lincolnshire Wildlife Trust and there is a nature trail in the grounds bounded by the River Bain.

16. Sir Joseph Banks Centre - Bridge Street

Sir Joseph Banks Centre

The Grade II listed building dates from the 18th century. It is the headquarters of the Sir Joseph Banks Society whose aim is to promote the achievements of Sir Joseph and to strengthen Lincolnshire's historic link with Australia and New Zealand. There is a courtyard at the rear of the premises which has been developed as a Tribute Garden to Sir Joseph Banks. It includes examples of many of the plants collected by him during his voyage on HMS Endeavour. There is also a well stocked shop providing information on Sir Joseph together with local art and craft work.

The building is open from 10 am to 4 pm Monday to Saturday and visitors are welcome to browse round the shop and garden. There is no entry charge.

17. Dr Edward Harrison's House - 30 West Street

West Street is a conservation area and many of the houses date back to Sir Joseph's period. Ignoring modern additions you can visualise a street that would have been familiar to Banks. There is a sculpture in tribute of Sir Joseph at the junction of West Street and the A158.

Dr Harrison who lived in number thirty, ran the Horncastle Dispensary and was also interested in psychology. From 1804 to 1821 there was a small unit in his garden where he observed and treated patients who were mentally disturbed. At a time when 'madness' was rarely considered a medical condition, he was caring for patients and developed treatments.

Dr Harrison was also instrumental in forming the Lincolnshire Benevolent Medical Society. At its first meeting at the Bull Hotel on 21st September 1804 he was elected President. The main aim of the Society was to reform medical practice and to eliminate quackery. In 1815 an Act of Parliament was eventually passed requiring the examination and licensing of apothecaries. This was mainly due to the activities of the Society and the support it received from Sir Joseph. His other major work was the treatment of spinal diseases and the founding of the Harrison Spinal Institution in London. Sir Joseph turned to Dr Harrison for treatment when gout disrupted his autumn sojourns at Revesby Abbey. He suffered his first attack in 1787 and on the 29th November he received a letter from George III:

'...The King is sorry to find Sir Joseph is still confined, and though it is the common mode to congratulate persons on the first fit of the Gout, He cannot join in so cruel an etiquette...'

In 1790 Sir Joseph suffered another attack and on 24th October Dorothea recorded one of the consequences in a letter to a friend:

'...instead of being able to fulfil our engagements we were soon obliged to return home, Sir Joseph having the Gout, which he has had very smartly in one foot and for two or three days was a little afraid of it in the other, but it has gone off very favourably and we were able to attend the Stuff Ball at Lincoln last Thursday, where we had a very great meeting, about 500 people there...'

Dr Harrison's House

During 1793 he suffered attacks of gout in January, May, June and finally in October during his visit to Revesby. Dorothea wrote to Miss Heber on 5th November:

'We attended the Stuff Ball October 23rd but were obliged to come home soon the next day, Sir Joseph being very indifferent with the gout. He has not been able to leave his room since, but is now much better that I have no doubt he will very soon get about again. We should have gone away this week and now hope to move early in next week. He don't like to fail attending the Royal Society if he can help it, this week it can't be helped.'

The bout was so severe it delayed his return to London until December. Dr Harrison made a number of visits to Revesby and applied treatments aimed at improving the circulation in his leg. The regime appears to have been effective as there were no further recorded bouts until 1795. Thereafter the pattern of the attacks became more regular and vicious, and during the last ten years of his life Banks was so severely crippled he had to use a wheelchair. Gout eventually prevented his annual visit to Revesby Abbey the last being the autumn of 1817 just three years before his death.

Sir John Franklin

1786 - 1853

(His achievements as Governor of Tasmania)

In England Sir John Franklin is best known for his Arctic exploration. He made several journeys to this icy outback the last resulting in his death. He is one of England's most celebrated explorers and Franklin's activities in the Arctic region are well documented. Sir Joseph was actively involved in these exploits as expressed by Captain John Ross in 1818 'you are the father of the Enterprise I have the honour to Command', and John Franklin was appointed to lead the expedition on the recommendation of Sir Joseph Banks. However, the six years he spent as Governor of Van Diemen's Land (Tasmania) have not received the same acknowledgement despite the important social changes he achieved.

John Franklin was born into a large family in 1786 and he resided in the small market town of Spilsby. Following a trip to Saltfleet when he was twelve years old John's ambition was a career in the Royal Navy. His first experience of naval life was on board HMS Polyphemus which took part in the Battle of Copenhagen. However the journey that was to have the most significant impact on his life was in 1801 when he sailed as midshipman on HMS Investigator under his cousin Matthew Flinders. During the long voyage to Australia Matthew explained the techniques of navigation and the skills required to survey and chart coastlines.

It proved to be a voyage of discovery that shaped his future. Franklin said of the experience

'...I imbibed the zeal of discovery... which in fact determined the whole character of my life.'

When Franklin was offered the governorship of Van Deimen's Land at the age of fifty he was reluctant to accept. He was persuaded only after receiving an assurance that this would not hinder his future naval career. He set sail from Southampton in 1836 accompanied by his wife Jane and daughter Eleanor arriving in January the following year.

Franklin's fame as an Arctic explorer preceded his arrival causing great excitement. He and his family were warmly received and balls, speeches and social events were organised in his honour. Settlers hoped their new Governor would be able to deliver changes that would improve conditions on the island. However Franklin did not have the authority to satisfy the settlers' demand of self-government and government officials did not support his liberal views.

His desire to rule by consensus was difficult when dealing with the harsh realities of a burgeoning colony. In 1837 Van Diemen's Land was one of the richest regions in Australia but despite this life was extremely hard. Self interest was the prevailing focus for settlers who were unable to influence the systems that governed their community.

Of the island's population of 42,000 in 1837 over 17,500 were convicts and they played a vital role in the development of Tasmania. When free settlers acquired land they were assigned convicts who worked for them, in turn the settlers took on the responsibility of providing discipline, work and sustenance for the prisoners. This greatly reduced the cost for the governing authority but the system lent itself to serious abuse. The Government finally abolished the system in 1841 and transportation ceased in 1853.

The island was originally named after the Governor General of Batavia. However its association with criminality and cruelty resulted in Franklin renaming it Tasmania in honour of the explorer Abel Tasman who discovered the island in 1642.

Franklin was the first Governor to consider Tasmania a permanent community rather than a temporary opportunity to exploit vested interests. There was growing pressure to reform the brutal penal discipline and settlers wanted more representation in the governing system. In his first year as Governor Franklin expressed his desire to see change. He believed that education and engendering a sense of community cohesion were vital in attaining improved social standards.

He made education one of his first priorities and in 1839 he laid his plan before the legislature. After much deliberation and many heated debates he overcame the fierce criticism his plans provoked and introduced the first state educational primary system in the British Empire.

Schools were to be founded where there were pupils in sufficient numbers able to attend. The cost was partly met by fees and partly by public funds. The government paid the schoolmaster's salary up to £100 a year, together with a grant of 10 shillings (50p.) per child per year once they exceeded the minimum number of attendees. The prescribed lessons were reading, writing and the four rules of arithmetic for boys while girls were instructed in needlework and knitting in preference to maths. The schools were non-denominational which overcame the varying demands of religious groups within the community. The initiative commenced in 1839 when rolls stood at 415 boys and 376 girls. A year later attendance had risen to 652 boys and 496 girls, the same increase as had occurred during the previous twelve year period.

Once basic education had been introduced Franklin turned his mind to more advanced studies. He revived a previously proposed college system to provide a more advanced curriculum for the brightest students. In 1840 Revd John Philip Gell arrived from England to take the post of lecturer in this new venture.

Not for the first time Franklin found himself at the centre of criticism but he refused to be daunted. He applied for a Charter and provided a ten acre site, the maximum he could acquire without requiring approval from the government in England. To ensure poorer members of the community were not excluded he created a state endowment to provide scholarships. Sadly he was recalled before he could establish the system and the Governor who succeeded him refused to support the project.

This, however, proved only a postponement as the proposal resurfaced. On this occasion it required the support of the public as the new Governor still refused state funding. Sir John donated £500 and Lady Franklin gave a valuable estate of 400 acres enabling the project to proceed. For a man who had tried to instil a sense of social awareness this community-led action must have given him great pleasure.

Education was not the only beneficiary during the Franklins' governorship. They also assisted organisations and events that brought people together. Science and natural history were of particular interest. A Horticultural Society was founded in Tasmania in 1839 and the Franklins were actively involved. He was a great supporter of the Land Scientific Society and increased the state grant to expand Tasmania's Botanic Gardens. The Mechanics' Institution in Hobart also received £100 a year from state funds under Franklin.

Sir John organised the island's first celebration on 1st December 1838 to commemorate the island's discovery by the Dutch navigator Abel Tasman. Although some scorned the idea it was a success attracting 12,000 people. The Hobart Regatta became an annual event and is still celebrated today.

The Franklins supported many organisations involved in cultural pursuits. They are particularly associated with the formation of the Tasmania Natural History Society and soon *after their arrival they started to make plans for the organisation. Unfortunately the Secretary of State was unsympathetic and forbade any state support. Undaunted they founded a museum at Lenah Valley from their own resources. Lady Jane donated the land and property which was turned into a natural history museum surrounded by native plants. It became a focus for those interested in furthering scientific development and the Franklins worked tirelessly to ensure its success.*

Franklin survived being shipwrecked on the Great Barrier Reef, the Battle of Trafalgar, and two Arctic expeditions. He was knighted in 1829 seven years before he and Lady Jane arrived in Australia. In Tasmania they regularly endured criticism yet despite this they carried out their duties, and greatly contributed to the social development of the island. They were actively involved and personally invested in many activities that created a firm foundation for future development. They led by example, and whenever possible they made community needs a priority in his Governorship.

Banksia Serrata

JOSEPH BANKS COUNTRY
Spilsby

Spilsby is one of Lincolnshire's smaller market towns and is situated on the edge of The Wolds an Area of Outstanding Natural Beauty. The town centre still largely adheres to the medieval street plan of four roads uniting in the extended market place. At one end stands the dignified bronze statue of the intrepid explorer Sir John Franklin at the other a graceful cross standing on 600 year old steps and base-stone.

The town is briefly mentioned in the Domesday Book and the market charter was obtained by the Lord of the Manor, Sir William de Willoughby in 1302. The weekly stock and food market was held on a Monday and the market continues to this day. During the mid 1700s a library was established by gentlemen of the town who met fortnightly at the White Hart to discuss new publications. In the late 18th century the Boston and Spilsby Bank was established surviving until 1814 when it became bankrupt.

Many craft and trades people lived and worked in the town. During the 18th century it was particularly well known as a producer of leather goods. It had boot and shoe makers, saddlers, glovers and tanners. The extent of the trade is indicated by the road named Leather Lane (now Queen Street). It would be here that the yards of tanners and curers together with people manufacturing finished merchandise could be found. In Pigot's Directory of 1822 the list of trades and crafts is extensive ranging from furniture to soap, tailor to maltster, stonemason to clockmaker. These merchants and the large markets selling sheep, cattle, fowl and rabbits together with produce that included eggs, cheese and vegetables were the backbone of the town's economy.

Today Spilsby is still dominated by its large market place surrounded by Georgian and Victorian buildings. The market continues but it does not bring the large crowds of yesteryear. There is a timeless atmosphere in the town and the scene is largely as it would have been during the life of Sir Joseph Banks and Sir John Franklin.

Franklin's Statue

Spilsby Town Trail

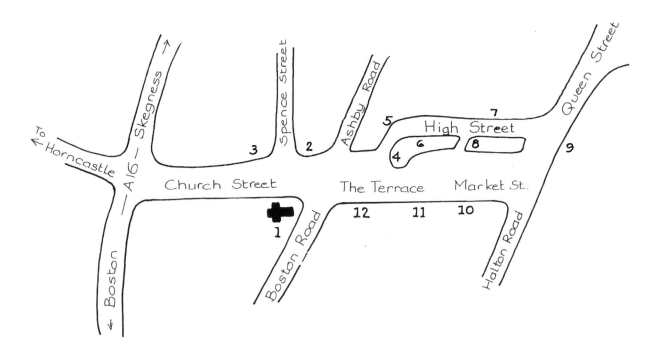

1. Church of St James

The church dates back to the 14th century although it underwent extensive rebuilding in 1879. At that time the green sandstone was faced with Ancaster stone, but surprisingly the tower was left unclad providing evidence of its original appearance.

In the 14th century an endowment was received providing a living for a Master and twelve priests. St James's became a collegiate church and in addition to religious duties the clerics provided educational opportunities within the community. These activities were suppressed during Henry VIII's reign in 1547 and the income from the endowment was used to found the Grammar School.

The church contains the Willoughby Chapel. This illustrious and highly influential family, who had links to the monarchy, have five magnificent tombs and two intricate brass tributes. The chapel is to the north of the altar and there is more information available in the church.

At the back of the church on the north wall there are three tablets commemorating three distinguished brothers of the Franklin family: James who made the first military survey of India, Willingham who became a Supreme Court Judge of Madras and John the Arctic explorer and Governor of Tasmania.

2. King Edward VI Grammar School - Church Road

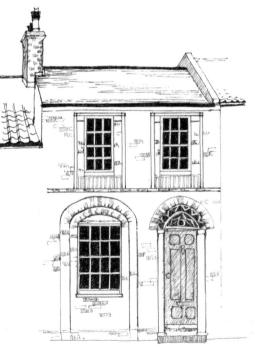

Opposite the church is the Grammar School, the middle section with the engraved stone lintel stating 'Grammar School 1550' is the oldest section of this attractive terrace. The building to the left was added in the 1600s and the attached house was erected in the Victorian period to provide living accommodation for the Headmaster. The most recent section was built in 1914 and is to the right of the original.

Section of Terrace

3. *Spilsby Theatre* - *Church Road*

This impressive building, formally the Sessions House, with its large columned entrance was built in 1826 by Henry Kendall. It replaced the old court-house in the Market Place and is now a Grade II listed building. This is all that remains of a substantial complex that included 250 cells and a police station. The prison itself survived only fifty years, but the court-house and police station were in use until 1984. The court-room now houses a theatre with seating for 90 people and there is a bar for patrons. In the cellar some of the prison cells survive and are used as changing rooms for artists.

Spilsby Theatre Entrance

4. *Franklin Statue* - *Market Place*

The statue of Spilsby's most famous son John Franklin is situated at the west end of the Market Place. It was unveiled in 1861 by Sir John Richardson, a doctor and botanist who sailed with Franklin on two occasions. Sir John Franklin is depicted holding his telescope in one hand while the other rests on an anchor. It also has a simple inscription 'Discoverer of the North West Passage and died in the Arctic regions, June 1847.' A public appeal to erect a tribute raised £750, and the celebrations included 500 buns for the children of the town, eighty old women received one ounce of tea and seventy-nine old men a pint of ale.

White Hart Inn

5. *White Hart Inn* - *High Street*

There has been a registered Inn on this site since 1660. The present building was altered during the 18th and 19th centuries and is a listed building. Banks attended meetings here to discuss opposition to the draining of Fen land. He chaired one such meeting in 1799 when seventy people were in attendance.

In 1790 the inn was a Mail Coach stop. At that time the journey from Louth to London took seventeen hours fifty-six minutes to cover the 155 miles from town to city. Here horses were changed and the coachman received refreshment before setting off on the next stage of the journey.

6. *Town Hall - High Street*

The Town Hall was built in 1764. The arches at ground level were open providing space for the weekly markets. This area has now been enclosed and is used by a number of businesses. The Court Room was located above the arches until it transferred to the Sessions House. The disused Court Room then became the Corn Exchange which operated until 1920. The end section of the Town Hall used to be the jail until it also moved to the new development in 1826.

Former Town Hall

Banks sat in the Court Room during the riots that occurred following increases in militia quotas during the Napoleonic war and fears of a French invasion. Unfortunately the public had mistakenly assumed that large numbers of men would be required to serve a minimum of five years and as a result riots occurred in several market towns including Spilsby.

7. *Franklin's House - High Street*

Franklin's House

This is now a bakery and on the wall there is a plaque explaining its connection with Franklin. He was the ninth child of twelve and two of his brothers also led distinguished lives. His father was apprenticed to a grocer and draper in Lincoln and opened a shop at these premises. The family lived above the shop and Sir John was born there. At the side of the building there is a narrow lane named Franklin Passage.

8. *Reverend Edward Walls House* - *High Street*

The house is on the opposite side of the street to Franklin's home. Edward Walls was a friend of Sir Joseph and they shared an interest in sheep breeding. He also attended Banks's fishing parties but sadly their friendship foundered when Walls became a strident voice against the costs of Fen drainage. Anonymous letters to the county newspapers were attributed to Revd Walls. He was a persistent critic and in exasperation Banks wrote a satirical poem 'A Mire Nymph' about the on-going problems:

Am I a prisoner to my deadly foes.
Has barbarous Banks prevailed
while worthy Walls.
In vain to rouse the tardy
Sokemen calls.

The Reverend Edward Walls House

9. *Methodist Chapel*

This large and impressive chapel faces the east market place and has a significant impact on the street scene. It was built in white brick in 1878 by Charles Bell and is flanked on either side by a manse.

10. *Red Lion* - *Market Place*

The income from this property, together with a close of pasture, was once endowed for the benefit of the poor of the Parish of Spilsby. In 1903 the gross yearly income was £40. Originally it was a single storey building as can been seen from the different brickwork on the upper floor

11. *Nelson Butt* - *Market Place*

This is another of the town's old inns and has an intriguing story. It is said that Nelson's body, preserved in brandy, was carried back to England in a barrel that was eventually given to the pub. The explanation suggested for its arrival in Spilsby is Franklin's presence at the Battle of Trafalgar when Nelson lost his life.

12. *The Terrace* - *Market Place*

The Terrace is a raised area with railings. Here there is an excellent row of Georgian town houses originally built for wealthy merchants of the town. It has been the home of vicars and doctors and was a familiar sight to Sir Joseph when he attended the Court Room and visited the White Hart Inn.

The Terrace

Red Lion Public House, Revesby

Almshouses, Revesby

Old Post Office, Revesby

Basket Weaver

JOSEPH BANKS COUNTRY
The Fens

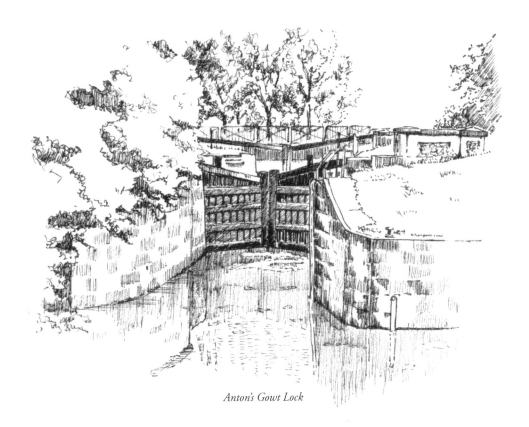

Anton's Gowt Lock

The northern Lincolnshire Fens are a low lying area which acted as a sump for the water running off the Wolds. The main occupations were fishing, wild fowling, harvesting reed and sedge for thatching and willow for basket weaving, and surrounding villages had common grazing rights over much of these Fens. Mosquitoes were abundant and 'Fen Ague', a local name for malaria, was a common ailment. To alleviate the symptoms residents used the Opium Poppy which grew wild in the county at that time.

In 1531 Henry VIII began a more organised attempt to tame the Fens by establishing Courts of Sewers. The members of a Court appointed local Commissioners who were responsible for maintaining and extending their local drainage system.

In the 1600s Dutch engineers introduced windmills with water scoops to the southern Fens, but a tax of 10 shillings (50p.) levied to help cover the cost of draining proved too expensive for many landowners. This necessitated funding from investors who were compensated with   a large share of the reclaimed land. The decision to enclose common land caused resentment eventually leading to riots, plundering of crops, and damage to the drainage system and property.

In 1642 Andrew Borrell gave a general description of the problems encountered in the Fens:

'It is a hard question whether the Sea or the Land Floods are the most potent enemies of the Fenns; but this is most certaine, that when the Sea floods and the Land floods meet, as they often times doe, halfe way betweixt the high Lands and the Sea, in that very place like two powerful enimies joining in one, they doe over-run the Levell, and drowne it from one end unto the other.'

At the turn of the 18th century, following a run of poor harvests the pressure to improve food production increased. This was further exacerbated by the Napoleonic war. Once again investment was required and to raise the necessary funds one third of common land in the East, West and Wildmore Fens was sold to finance the drainage scheme. The remaining land was divided between the participating parishes and then sub-divided between parishioners holding commoners' rights. The draining of Fen land was eventually successful converting it into rich agricultural land.

Like his father Sir Joseph was actively involved in promoting waterways and drainage systems in Lincolnshire. In 1799 he began investigating the possibility of improving land north of Boston. He chaired a meeting at the Bull Hotel in Horncastle in December 1800. It was agreed that John Rennie, a Scottish engineer, be asked to survey East, West and Wildmore Fens and produce a new gravity drainage system. One of the Acts stated:

'An Act for the better and more effectually draining certain tracts of land called Wildmore Fen and the West and East Fens in the County of Lincoln, and also the low lands and grounds in the several parishes, townships and places having Rights of Common on the said Fens and other low lands and grounds lying contiguous or adjacent thereto.' (1801)

As a result the Witham Fourth Internal Drainage Board was established covering an area of more than 40,000 acres.

Opium Poppy

Some drains also served as navigable canals significantly improving the transport infrastructure, prior to railways. As a consequence of these actions the landscape changed in character and employment patterns shifted to accommodate the prevailing conditions.

This car tour takes you through a part of the Fen where the Banks and Rennie partnership had significant impact. It provides the opportunity to take short walks or visit local inns and tea rooms.

Hagnaby Lock

Start at Revesby. Take the Revesby/Boston road (B1183) until you come to a small bridge. Take the turning to Hagnaby Lock at the side of the bridge.

1. The West Fen catchwater drain flows east beneath Revesby Bridge on its way to Hagnaby Lock. The road is higher than field level a feature of many roads on this tour, and is the result of being built on the spoil banks created by digging the drains. Drains like this were kept clear by a gang of men forming a chain, then passing the silt and clay from spade to spade up the bank. It was called Jackballing. In 1919 to receive full pay each man had to remove two cubic yards of clay a day.

   Continue along this road until you come to the lock.

2. Hagnaby Lock was one of many locks built across the Fens. This one was used to control the water level and provide navigation to Boston. The brick bridge is in the style of Rennie.

   Prior to drainage areas such as this would have been inundated with water. The meres, rivers and dikes provided eel, pikes and roach in huge numbers and water birds in flocks of a size unimaginable today. Lincolnshire provided food for the gentry across the country. Before enclosure the East Fen was said to have supplied 31,000 mallard, widgeon and teal for the London market. The Fen also produced thousands of pecks of cranberries and families in the county were very familiar with the taste of cranberry tart.

   Turn right over the bridge and follow the road.

3. Not far from the lock on the right, is Hagnaby Fen Nature Area. A path leads to a hide overlooking a flood area that covers 7.5 ha and is capable of holding 70,000 cubic metres of water. It gives a glimpse of the Fen landscape as it would have been

in Sir Joseph's youth. As a result of drainage wetland habitats were lost and many species became extinct in Lincolnshire, a fact regretted by Banks later in his life.

Joseph spent much of his youth rowing boats across meres and ponds exploring the rivulets and islands in the East Fen. In his teenage years his father introduced him to his friend the Earl of Sandwich who was to become First Lord of the Admiralty in 1763 and 1771 to 1782. In that capacity he helped Banks establish his many contacts in the Royal Navy and supported the expeditions and explorations that he initiated.

Hagnaby Lock, Nature Reserve

A passage written in the 1790s by Arthur Young, Secretary of the Board of Agriculture, who was a regular visitor and correspondent of Sir Joseph, gives a description of Wildmore Fens prior to drainage:

'Whole acres are covered with thistles and nettles, four feet high and more. There are men that have vast number of geese, even to 1000 and more... There may be five sheep an acre kept in summer on Wildmore and West fens, besides many horses, young cattle and geese; if there are any person who profit, it is those people who keep geese... Upon driving West fen in 1784 there were found, 16th and 17th September, 3,936 head of horned cattle. In dry years it is perfectly white with sheep... In East fen are 2,000 acres of water... Sir Joseph Banks had the goodness to order a boat and accompanied me into the heart of this fen, which in the wet season had the appearance of a chain of lakes, bordered by great crops of reeds... It is in general from three to four feet deep in water, and in one place, a channel between two lakes, five to six feet...'

At the end of the road turn left onto the A16 and immediately right into the East Fen Catchwater Drain Road.

4. The A16 follows the line of the glacial moraine that raised it above the water level. This was a

Geese

Junction of Bell Water and Hobhole Drains (Duke of Wellington Pub)

path through the Fen prior to drainage. It connected islands, represented today by villages such as Stickney and Sibsey which were situated above sea level.

The main occupation in the three Fens was harvesting the natural resources provided by the water that surrounded them. To protect the Fens and those with commoners' rights there were many byelaws. For example no foreigner, that is anybody who did not live in the Fens, could fish or take wildfowl at any time. 'All night' fowling could only be conducted between the hours of 8pm and 2am and no fowl was to be taken during the breeding period. No swan, crane, or bittern eggs, or any other eggs except duck and geese were allowed to be collected. During the summer the water receded leaving huge stretches of land that produced excellent grazing for animals. In the West and Wildmore Fen sheep and cattle had to be branded before grazing on this silt land.

Turn left into Scarborough Road in the direction of Midville and on reaching a bridge cross the Hobhole drain and then turn right over the Bell Water Drain.

5.   An ideal stopping place is near the Duke of Wellington, parts of which date back to around 1812. Nearby there is a confluence of drains merging with a major drain, the Hobhole on its way to Boston and the sea. This used to be a busy waterway with packet boats and barges taking passengers and goods to Boston. The fourteen mile long Hobhole was the most costly and controversial part of Rennie's scheme.

There is a brick bridge believed to be the original built by Rennie and two recent bridges constructed of concrete.

Continue travelling south towards Midville crossing the former railway with the station nearby. It was opened in 1913 and operated until 1970. When railways were first introduced many considered them a complementary method of transport rather than a competitor to navigation. Further along the road there is St Peter's Church built in 1819.

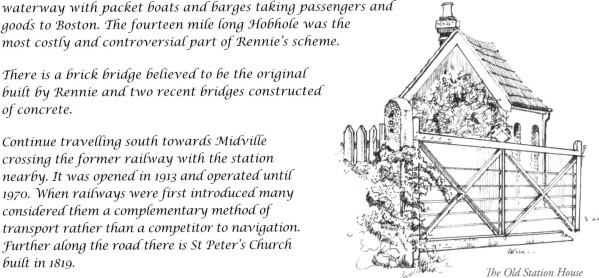

The Old Station House

6. *Midville and nearby Eastville are two Fen parishes created after drainage under the new Township Act of 1812. They were established to enable the newly acquired agricultural land to be farmed, and to provide services for those operating and using the waterways.*

Prior to the canals goods were transported by horse and cart, a slow journey with limited capacity. Barges overcame this constraint providing an inexpensive method of bulk transport. It enabled coal to be imported into the county, an important cargo for Lincolnshire as it provided opportunities for industry to develop. In some large towns coal was used to produce gas which lit streets and buildings.

Lade Bank Pumping Station

Continue to the 'T' junction turn left in the direction of New Leake and immediately right onto Hobhole Bank towards Lade Bank Pumping Station.

7. *Lade Bank Pumping Station was built in 1867. Following drainage an unforeseen problem was land shrinkage and in a short time it dropped by two feet causing insufficient fall in the Hobhole. Also in times of heavy rainfall the East Fen became flooded.*

Steam pumps were installed at Lade Bank with six coal fired boilers to operate a pair of 240hp engines. In 1872 these pumps lifted 18 million gallons of water out of the East Fen. In 1940 they were replaced with diesel engines that were housed in a new building. These are still used in extreme conditions; today however the electric pump installed in 1963 is the usual method of control.

The chimney is part of the original boiler house and is a listed structure. The Dutch-made weed-cleaner can still be seen. It prevented debris getting into the pumps. Between the old and new buildings are the lock gates used by packet boats taking passengers to and from Boston market.

Continue south in the direction of Sibsey crossing the East Lincolnshire railway. At the crossroads turn right following the Sibsey sign onto the B1184 at Benington Bridge.

8. At this point you can stop and admire the extent of one of the major drains and navigational waterways through the Fens – The Hobhole. It stretches in a straight line from Toynton Fenside in the north to the River Witham in the south and is fourteen miles long.

    This was hand dug and it took hundreds of navvies using spades, barrows and planks. Normally the work was done during the winter when agricultural labourers were available. A network of wooden planks and decking enabled the clay laden barrows to be taken up the new banks. Steam pumps helped to keep working sections free of water. One 6hp pump manufactured by James Watt and Boulton was purchased for £324 and was worked so hard it lasted only three months. It was dangerous and exhausting work in very unpleasant conditions.

Iron Bridge, designed by Rennie

Continue along the B1184 over a level crossing towards Sibsey. At the junction turn right onto the A16 and first left onto the B1184 in the direction of Frithville. On reaching the Frithville junction turn left onto the B1183 towards Boston along the West Fen Drain.

9. The six-sailed Sibsey Trader Windmill built in 1877 is open weekends from March to November and has a tea room.

The principal reason for Sir Joseph's determination to see the Lindsey Fens drained was the desire to increase food production. By the late 1790s agriculture was in crisis and corn had become scarce and expensive. This was further exacerbated by the Napoleonic war. The result was severe shortages and high prices bringing great distress. During this very difficult period Sir Joseph organised shipments of rice which arrived at the port in Boston. He instructed James Roberts at Revesby to distribute the rice to his tenants and thoughtfully included cooking instructions for the recipients.

Continue towards Boston following the canal past the turning to Boston Golf Club. In doing so you will be crossing a bridge which is another Rennie construction. Park near the graceful Iron Bridge which is a listed structure.

10. *This area contains a complex system of drains that carry the water from the Fens and the Wolds on its way to the sea. Much of this system can be seen from a public footpath that goes through the golf course - the walk takes approximately twenty minutes.*

Lock Gates

John Rennie's system entailed separating the Wolds water from the Fens. He ran the Wolds water into Catchwater Drains which fed by an aquaduct into the Maud Foster Drain. The Fen water was fed into a network of larger drains that emptied into the Hobhole Drain. By 1814 the East, West and Wildmore Fens were fit for agriculture.

From the Iron Bridge walk back towards the golf course and enter at the footway sign. Carefully cross the course and follow the drain north. From the bridge you can see the lock gates built in the early 1800s to control the Fen water. It took nearly 14 million bricks to build the necessary sluices and bridges that eventually tamed the marsh land.

Cross the bridge and follow the water's edge. You can turn back at any point or continue in a circle arriving back at the Iron Bridge.

From the Iron Bridge drive back towards the Rennie Bridge and take the Anton's Gowt road on the left (Gowt is an old Lincolnshire word meaning 'go-out'). Follow it into the village and park in the vicinity of the Royal Oak. Anton's Gowt is a delightful stop providing information boards, public path and picnic tables.

11. Follow the path that runs past the lock gates opposite the pub. The lock provides boat access between the Newham Drain and the River Witham which has a water level several feet higher.

The banks of the Witham were heightened and fourteen meanders were straightened on the route from Lincoln to Boston. The work was completed in 1766. It was at Anton's Gowt that Sir Joseph's annual fishing parties stopped to cook and eat their catch on their way from Dogdyke to Boston. These were grand affairs that lasted three or four days and involved a number of boats.

In September 1790 a letter written by Dorothea Banks describes this annual event:

'We had but indifferent weather for our fishing party. Three days it was very showery and one day very fine. Our boat is very long and broad and our awning is so stout and we have plenty of room that we are not afraid of a little rain. We are very warm when shut up in the evening. A great deal of fish was caught, and we had a very large party. The gentlemen were out early in the morning, and the ladies met about noon.'

Sir Joseph also kept records of the fishing parties. In 1788 he noted that they were a party of twenty-five and they ate 3.5 lbs of pike, 32 lbs of perch, 5.75 lbs of eels, 19.5 lbs of salmon and 0.5 lbs of flounders.

Sir Joseph and John Rennie created a water system that changed forever the landscape of the Fens. Many mourned the loss of the wetlands which provided a habitat for now extinct species in Lincolnshire and destroyed a way of life that had survived for centuries. Fen land was replaced by rich agricultural land that supported a more profitable farming system and improved the infrastructure for travel and transport. These watercourses created over two hundred years ago remain at the heart of modern day drainage in the Boston area. Some mechanisation has taken place but the pattern of water movement remains the same as that created by John Rennie and supported by Sir Joseph Banks.

Water Vole

The Picnic

JOSEPH BANKS COUNTRY

Boston

Boston Quayside

Records of the area we now know as Boston can be traced back to the 7th century, when legend claims a monk named Botolph built himself a hut and brought religion to the inhospitable marshland. The settlement does not appear in the Domesday Survey as its development commenced some twenty years later. In 1545 Henry VIII granted the town a Charter and it became a Borough. Boston continued to grow, becoming an important trading post and the second largest port in the country.

Sir Joseph was granted the Freedom of the Borough in 1771 and became Recorder of Boston in 1808. Pishey Thompson's 'History of Boston' was dedicated to Banks. He received copies of engravings and was regularly updated on the book's progress until its publication in 1820, the same year as Banks died.

Sir Joseph was also a friend of the Fydell family who were highly influential in the town. With their assistance he organised the annual Fishing Party on the Witham, an event Sir Joseph particularly looked forward to during his visits to Lincolnshire.

The fortune of medieval Boston declined as wool manufacture contracted, but recovered with the railways in 1848 and the opening of the dock in 1884. Today it is one of Lincolnshire's larger towns and has a busy street market on Wednesdays and Saturdays, a scene that would have been familiar to Sir Joseph.

The old world charm still exists and many areas have changed little over the centuries. As you walk this trail you will see buildings which existed during Sir Joseph's lifetime.

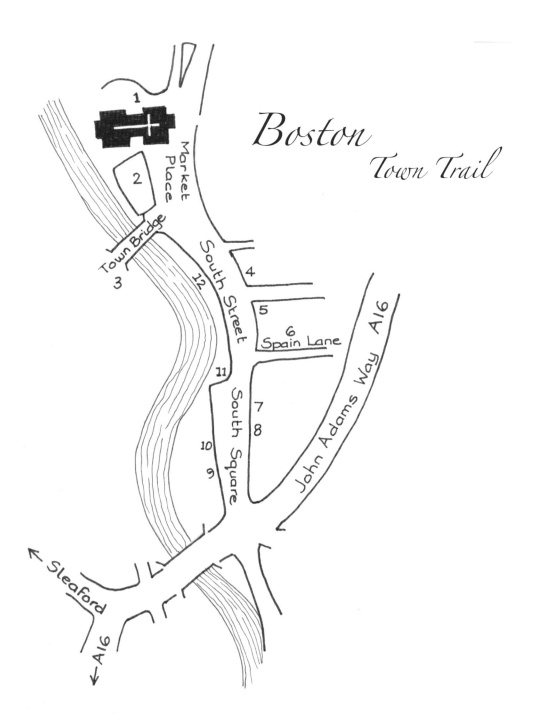

Boston
Town Trail

1. *Church of St Botolph affectionately known as The Stump*

St Botolph's is named after the monk who settled here in the 7th century. The foundation stone was laid in 1309 and it is one of the largest parish churches in England. Wool made Boston great and the church was built with profits from that trade. It has a lantern tower where fires were lit to guide ships up the Haven to the quayside and gave direction to people crossing the surrounding Fen land. The church has a fascinating history and there are excellent guide books in the shop.

Memorials associated with Sir Joseph and Australia:

- In the north aisle the Fydell family are commemorated on the east wall. They were close friends of Sir Joseph.

- In the tower there is a wall plaque commemorating the founders of Australia.

    1. Sir Joseph Banks who throughout his life offered support and advice to governors and individuals.

    2. James Roberts and Peter Briscoe from Revesby who sailed with Banks on the Endeavour.

    3. George Bass who explored and mapped areas of Australia.

    4. Matthew Flinders who circumnavigated the continent and mapped its coastline.

    5. Sir John Franklin who was Governor of Tasmania and established the country's first educational system.

All these men were born in Lincolnshire. The plaque was unveiled by the acting High Commissioner of Australia towards the end of 1945.

Opposite the memorial to the Lincolnshire founders of Australia is a tribute to some of the most prominent Boston Puritans. They played an important role in the founding and governance of America's Massachusetts Bay Colony. Thomas Dudley, Richard Bellingham, John Leverett and Simon Bradstreet served the colony as governors or deputy governors for all but four of its first fifty-six years.

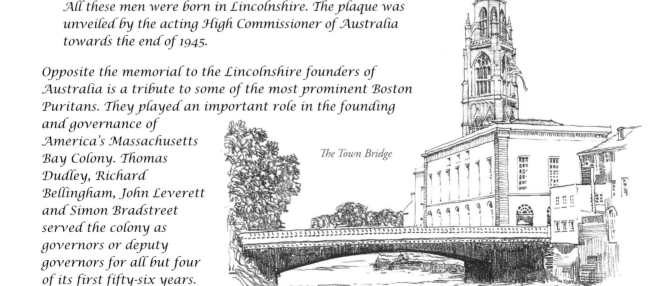

The Town Bridge

2. *Corporation Building* – Market Place

This large three storey building bears the town's coat of arms. It was built in 1772 to replace the Guildhall and served as the Town Hall and Court Room. The arches were originally open on both sides giving direct access to the river where fish was unloaded, and the town's Market Square. The markets operated in the space between the arches. It remained the Town Hall and Court Room until 1882 when it was replaced by the Assembly Rooms.

Sir Joseph, as Recorder of Boston, would have attended court and taken part in meetings here. One such occasion was April 1800 when Banks chaired a meeting of landowners with interests in the East, West and Wildmore Fens. It was agreed that a subscription list be opened to cover the fees incurred in obtaining an Act of Parliament.

Corporation Building

In 1801 Banks again chaired a meeting to discuss concerns relating to the costs of the proposed drainage and the implications contained in John Rennie's report proposing a new gravity drainage system.

3. *Town Bridge* – off Market Place

There has been a ferry or bridge near this site for centuries. In 1806 John Rennie designed a graceful iron bridge as part of the new drainage and navigation system, but in 1913 it was replaced by the present Town Bridge. A plaque acknowledges Rennie's design of the earlier structure.

4. ## Custom House - South Street

The present building replaced a previous one on the same site. The building we see today was erected in 1725 at a cost of £365. It is the second oldest Custom House in England and has the Royal Coat of Arms above the door. During the 1800s smuggling flourished, and on one occasion in 1823 it took four wagons to remove smuggled goods to the Custom House.

Custom House

5. ## The Guildhall - South Street

Parts of the building date back to 1390. The banqueting hall still has its 15th century roof and its west window still contains the original stained glass. In 1545, Henry VIII bestowed a Charter on the town and it was the first Town Hall for the new Corporation. It had a Council Chamber and Court Room on the first floor with a chapel, cells and a large kitchen on the ground floor.

Nearly 2,000 petty criminals from Lincolnshire were transported to Australia. Banks first suggested the continent as a suitable colony for petty felons in 1779. In May 1787 the first ships sailed from London to Botany Bay with 564 men and 192 women on board together with crew, troops and a large contingent of officials. One of the passengers was the Judge Advocate and he commented:

Boston Quayside

'we were leaving the world behind us to enter into a state unknown'.

In 1809, following Banks's appointment as Recorder of Boston the corporation commissioned his portrait. It was painted by Thomas Phillips and was hung in the Guildhall in 1814. The building has been Boston's Museum since 1929.

6. ## Sam Newsom Centre - South Street

This was originally a warehouse built about 1800 by Thomas Fydell. He imported wine from France and may well have supplied Sir Joseph's cellar at Revesby Abbey. The warehouse has now been converted into a music centre providing teaching facilities and a concert venue for the community.

7. *Packhouse Quayside* - South Street

There is an excellent information board on the quayside. The steps down to the river and the positions of the hoists used for loading and unloading boats can still be seen. The stout poles in the river bed protected moored boats from the stone wall. The tidal river provided the opportunity for international trade particularly with the Hanseatic League traders in the Baltic. Wool, cloth, hides, lead and salt were exported whilst wine from France, iron from Sweden and fish and furs from the Baltic were imported.

8. *Warehouses* - South Square

During the Industrial Revolution the movement of people from the countryside to industrial centres meant large quantities of grain and other food produce were transported from Lincolnshire to cities in the Midlands. As trade increased more warehouses were built between the river and South Square to store grain, wool and other products. Many have been demolished but some have been converted into flats.

The River Witham was straightened and the Grand Sluice opened in 1766. The river from Chapel Hill to Boston was straightened reducing its length from seventeen miles to eleven. The sluice controlled the River Witham enabling water levels to remain high and the river navigable. When the water was released at the sluice it helped to remove the silt in the Haven giving access to larger ships.

9. *Magnet Tavern* - South Square

Dating back to the 1700s, this was once the home of the Weight family who were solicitors and merchants in the town. They also owned many grain warehouses. The house was converted to a pub in the mid-1800s.

Tribute to Cook's Endeavour Voyage behind Fydell House

10. *Fydell House* – *South Square*

The house is named after the well known Boston family who purchased it in 1726. At the bottom of the garden with its trimmed box and yew topiary there is a tribute to Sir Joseph. Canon A.M. Cook wrote about the history of Boston and his verses about Sir Joseph are engraved on the four sides of the plinth. It was unveiled in 1997 by the High Commissioner of Australia who visited the town when the replica of the Endeavour was moored in Boston Dock. The ships arrival proved so popular people had to queue for hours before being able to board. The Endeavour replica made two further visits to Boston.

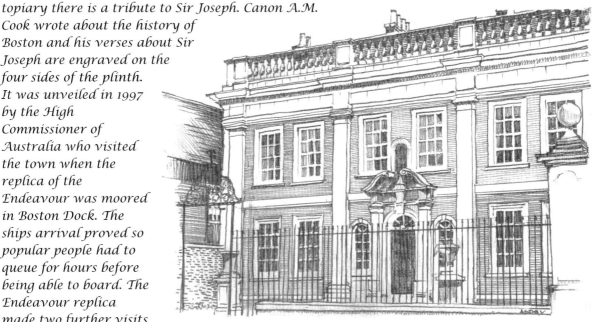

Fydell House

Four members of the Fydell family were Mayors of Boston and three were also Members of Parliament. They were close friends of Sir Joseph and in 1777 and 1782 they tried unsuccessfully to persuade Banks to become the Corporation's representative in Parliament.

The Fydell family also attended the annual fishing parties on the Witham organised by Banks between 1784 and 1796. These took place at the beginning of September and continued for three or four days with two or three dozen guests participating. The river was systematically fished with Seine nets seventy yards long and twenty feet deep which were stretched across the river and were pulled by a horse on each bank. Behind the nets the boats followed, the smaller ones conveying the servants who managed the hauling of the net and the landing of fish. The nets were hauled ten to twelve times a day with an average daily catch of 300-400 pounds of fish. The boat hire cost Banks eleven guineas and the nets three guineas.

They sailed each day from Dogdyke stopping at Anton's Gowt at around five o'clock. Here servants organised the portable iron stoves and large fish kettles. They cooked mostly pike, perch and eels, but occasionally included chub, bream, salmon or flounders. Guests consumed between one and two pounds of fish each. They arrived at the Grand Sluice in Boston at approximately nine-thirty in the evening.

Dorothea Banks provides an insight into these gatherings in a letter dated 17th September 1794:

'We then went out on our annual fishing party, which lasted four days. We were during the time at a friend's house in Boston, had three days good, and one day so bad we only went down late to dine with the gentlemen. When in our boat we are very secure, it's a great barge, and our awning is strong and high, so its like sitting in a great tent...'

11. Spain Lane - Off South Street

The large building on the south side was built in the 1700s and provided four homes. Blackfriars Theatre and Arts Centre is housed in the remains of a Dominican Friary refectory dating back to the 13th century. Spain Court consists of twelve charming Regency cottages and it is paved with York stone and has a cobbled road.

Spain Court

12. Shodfriars - South Square

An attractive black and white Tudor style building. It was extensively and elaborately remodelled in the 1870s with a second front gable. The architects were two sons of the distinguished architect Sir George Gilbert Scott.

13. Boston Woods Trust - Wyberton South of the town

The aim is to plant a 3,000 acre belt of trees from Wyberton to Boston. It is to include a 180 acre country park dedicated to Sir Joseph Banks and an arboretum featuring trees from across the world. Seventy nine acres have already been developed and includes a wild flower meadow and mixed woodland.

Transportation from Lincolnshire to Australia

1787 - 1853

The process of deporting undesirable people to foreign lands was established long before Sir Joseph suggested Australia as a suitable penal colony. In 1598 a law was passed which stated:

'Rogues appearing dangerous to the inferior sort of people or such as will not be reformed of their roguish kind of life are to be banished out of this realm... and conveyed to such parts beyond the seas as shall be at any time hereafter assigned for that purpose by the Privy Council.'

In the 17th century this definition was extended to include vagrants and thousands were sent to plantations in the West Indies as labourers for settlers. After the 1718 Transportation Act the numbers deported to America increased dramatically but after the American Declaration of Independence in 1776 convicts were refused entry.

English jails were soon overflowing with no sustainable solution to the chronic overcrowding. In 1799 Sir Joseph Banks suggested to a House of Commons committee that Botany Bay in Australia would be a suitable penal colony. Seven years later preparations began and Captain Arthur Phillip was appointed to command a fleet of ships to transport convicts to the Australian continent. The fleet sailed in May 1787 arriving in Botany Bay in January 1788 with 756 prisoners on board. Botany Bay proved an unsuitable location so Port Jackson, now Sydney became the first penal colony.

Sir Joseph maintained close contact with developments in Australia. In a letter to Governor Hunter he requested him to offer encouraging words to two young men from a village near Revesby. They had been transported for maiming a cow, Sir Joseph said:

'tell them that by continuing a good conduct they may some time revisit their country and their friends.'

Transportation to Australia continued unabated until 1840 when New South Wales refused to accept convicts. Between 1844 and 1849 nine ships transporting people labelled 'Exiles' arrived *in Port Phillip. These former prisoners had undergone a period of probation in England and were classified as 'Assisted Immigrants'. Once they had landed they were free to establish a new life in Australia.*

The beautiful Norfolk Island was established as a penal colony to cope with the problem of convicts who broke the law in Australia. Fifteen ships carrying Australian offenders landed there between 1840 to 1850. As the majority of prisoners were re-offenders the regime was particularly harsh and brutal.

Of prisoners transported from Lincolnshire 784 went directly to New South Wales, 798 to Van Diemen's Land (now Tasmania) and 131 to Western Australia. The remaining convicts were transported to Port Phillip, Geelong, Norfolk Island and Moreton Bay. Assisted Immigrants and convicts with conditional pardons or certificates of freedom arrived as prospective citizens of Australia.

An excellent guide to the number of Lincolnshire people transported is contained in a register of convicts, many of them petty felons, providing details of 1,800 people who left our shores for the new continent. It lists the name, age, date of sentence, sentencing district, length of sentence, where they lived, year deported, destination, and the name of the ship. The detailed record of each person in the register provides a direct link between Lincolnshire and the continent of Australia. It can be found on the Lincolnshire County Council website.

Matthew Flinders

1774-1814

Matthew Flinders, born 16th March 1774, was the first child of a respected country surgeon. He attended the Free School in his native village Donington then moved to Horbling Grammar School where he completed his education. His father had hoped that he would follow him into the medical profession but Matthew was determined to seek a career at sea. When his father finally relented Matthew joined the Royal Navy in 1789 as a Lieutenant's Servant.

Two years later he sailed as a midshipman on HMS Providence under Captain William Bligh who was undertaking a second successful voyage to transport breadfruit from Tahiti to Jamaica. The first had been the fateful Bounty expedition. It was under Bligh that Matthew learned navigation and was given the opportunity to draw his first charts. Both voyages had been initiated and supported by Sir Joseph Banks.

In February 1795 Matthew, his twelve year old brother Samuel, and a close friend George Bass who was the ship's surgeon, sailed on HMS Reliance. When they arrived in Australia Captain John Hunter commenced his term as Governor of New South Wales.

In 1798 Governor Hunter assigned HMS Norfolk to Flinders. It was a thirty-five foot vessel based on a longboat. His orders to Flinders were to establish whether or not there was a channel separating New South Wales and Van Diemen's Land. The expedition discovered that there was a passage and to honour his Lincolnshire friend Flinders requested that it be named Bass Strait. This was in recognition of George Bass's earlier exploration of the area which indicated the existence of the channel. Flinders went on to circumnavigate the island which was later renamed Tasmania. He returned to England in August 1800 having been away five and a half years.

One of his first tasks on his return was to send a letter on the 6th September 1800 to Sir Joseph Banks who received it at his Derbyshire estate, Overton Hall, two days later. Flinders also dedicated his book entitled 'Observations on the Coast of Van Diemen's Land, on Bass Strait and its Islands' to Banks. This enabled him to maintain contact with Banks and provided the opportunity to explain his desire to explore coastal areas round New South Wales. The purpose was to determine whether New Holland and New South Wales were separate islands, or parts of one great continent.

Banks was enthusiastic and successfully persuaded his friend Earl Spencer, then First Lord of the Admiralty, to organise an expedition. After a few months at home Flinders was offered the command of HMS Investigator. In February 1801 preparations were underway for a voyage that would ultimately propel Flinders to fame in Australia.

During the Investigator's refit Sir Joseph persuaded the Navy to make modifications aimed at helping plants survive the long journey back to England. He also successfully requested that naturalist Robert Brown, Ferdinand Bauer, a botanical artist, and William Westall, a landscape artist, be allowed to join the crew. He sponsored these men and helped organise all necessary equipment required by them to accomplish their commission.

The crew also included Matthew's nineteen year old brother Samuel, Robert Fowler of Horncastle who later rose to the rank of Vice Admiral, and fifteen year old midshipman John Franklin who would become famous for his Arctic exploits. When Matthew was eleven years old his father married his second wife and she was related to the Franklins of Spilsby. The young Franklin boys and Matthew became great friends and he wrote long letters to them when at sea.

While preparations were being made for the voyage Matthew received invitations to Revesby Abbey where Sir Joseph would introduce him as 'my own countryman'. During this period Matthew had married Ann Chappelle of Partney hoping that she would be allowed to accompany him to New South Wales. Unfortunately this desire was dashed when the Navy refused permission. In July 1801 following only three months of marriage Matthew joined HMS Investigator.

In December they arrived at Cape Leeuwin on the south-west coast and Flinders became the fourth navigator to land on this largely unexplored area of New Holland's coast. He landed at King George's Sound for repairs and the survey of the southern coastline commenced. Disaster struck at a point subsequently named Cape Catastrophe. Seven crew members, and the Master, John Thistle, were drowned. Flinders erected a memorial to them at Memory Cove and named nearby islands after those who had died. Other places were named after Lincolnshire towns and villages including Cape Donington, Boston Island, Louth Bay, Point Bolingbroke, Partney Island and Spilsby Island.

They continued to Port Lincoln, Spencer Gulf and the Gulf of St Vincent where they discovered Kangaroo Island. They then sailed on to Port Phillip arriving at Port Jackson (Sydney) in May 1802, having travelled 20,000 miles. HMS Investigator underwent a three month overhaul after which Flinders sailed north along the difficult east coast encountering the Great Barrier Reef. He found a route through this hazard and it became known as Flinders Passage.

Passing through the Torres Strait, he mapped the Gulf of Carpentaria but by that time the Investigator was rotting so badly he had to make a dash for port. He covered the 5,000 miles to Port Jackson in two months. At the end of his coastal journeys Matthew Flinders became the first navigator to circumnavigate Australia.

Like many explorers Flinders experienced perilous situations, some physical, some political. His return journey proved disastrous. HMS Investigator was deemed unseaworthy so he took passage to Europe on HMS Porpois commanded by Robert Fowler of Horncastle. Just 750 miles into the journey, at a point north east of Port Jackson, the boat was shipwrecked on a sandbank at Wreck Reef. Matthew with twelve members of the crew successfully made the hazardous journey back to the mainland in the ship's six oared cutter. He organised his return to Wreck Reef with three rescue vessels six weeks later. The remaining crew had endured those weeks marooned on the sandbank. By what seemed a miracle all returned safely to the mainland.

Following this remarkable rescue Flinders resumed his journey to England as commander on HMS Cumberland. However the ship leaked so badly he had to land at Mauritius in 1803. Unfortunately his passport was for passage on HMS Investigator creating a difficult political wrangle. England was at war with France and Mauritius was under French control. As a consequence Flinders and John Aken, who had been master of HMS Investigator, found themselves branded spies and imprisoned.

Two years later Aken was released and took with him Flinders's sixteen charts and a journal of his journey up to March 1803. When Matthew realised he was to remain a prisoner he continued writing a narrative of his voyage from Port Jackson and recording his observations on compass deviation.

During Matthew's incarceration Sir Joseph Banks maintained contact with Ann Flinders updating her on attempts to free him. In June 1805 he wrote to Matthew informing him of his correspondence with his wife. Following representations and negotiation the order for Flinders release was signed in Paris on 11th March 1806. Banks wrote to Ann informing her that letters had been sent requesting Matthew's release. However, despite continuous efforts it took another four years before Flinders finally arrived in England during October 1810 a very sick man.

Climbing the rigging

His observations on compass deviation resulted in a series of experiments with ships in home waters in 1812. Flinders recorded his findings and eventually the Lords Commissioners of the Navy accepted his memorandum. With an arrangement of soft iron bars above the compass needle he eliminated compass deviation caused by the ship's magnetism. The Flinders Bar became standard equipment throughout the world. The design of the Bar was modified in the 19th century by Lord Kelvin but the principle remained the same and it is still fitted to ships in the 21st century.

One of the Admiralty's original instructions to Flinders in 1801 was to publish details of his journey on HMS Investigator. Compilation of A Voyage to Terra Australis commenced in January 1811. Sir Joseph assigned the title but it was a footnote made by Flinders in the introduction to Volume I that provided the continent with its name:

'Had I permitted myself any innovation upon the original term, it would have been to convert it into Australia, as being more agreeable to the ear, and an assimilation to the names of the other great portions of the earth.'

A Voyage to Terra Australis was in two volumes. The first contained 200 pages of discoveries prior to the Investigator together with details of departure through to arrival at Port Jackson in 1802. The second volume completes the journey of circumnavigation and provides details of the homeward journey and imprisonment. Appendices include detailed information on compass deviation and a study by Robert Brown on the taxonomy and distribution of plants collected during exploration. Of Bauer's 1,500 sketches, ten were selected as well as nine of Westall's illustrations. In addition there were sixteen charts and two pages of costal profiles.

A Voyage to Terra Australis was published only days before Matthew Flinders died on the 19th July 1814 at the young age of 40. Following his death his wife and daughter endured many years of financial hardship. When the colonies of New South Wales and Victoria became aware of Ann's situation they secured her a pension in recognition of Matthew's contribution to the new continent. News of this acknowledgement did not reach Ann before she died in 1852. Her daughter Ann accepted the pension which she used to educate Matthew's grandson. He was to become Sir William Matthew Flinders Petrie, a famous Egyptologist and Professor at the University of London.

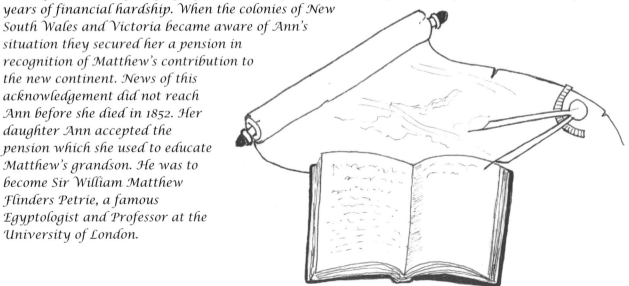

Matthew did not receive the acknowledgement he deserved in England but he did become a legend in Australia where he is known as Flinders the Navigator. His achievements are celebrated by countless tributes to him. There are memorials and his name has been given to streets, institutions and universities and projects and challenges are named after him. All these are testaments to his pioneering spirit and the lasting impact his exploration had on what was then a largely uncharted continent.

Flax Field

JOSEPH BANKS COUNTRY
Donington

Flinders Statue

Donington was a thriving market town even before it was recorded in the Domesday Book. It was built at the junction between Holland Causeway coming from Spalding and the well used Roman road Salter's Way from Wainfleet. In the Roman period pack horses carrying salt would slowly make their way along the track after crossing Bicker Haven just two miles from Donington. These routes provided the town with an early foundation as a distribution centre.

Charters to hold markets were granted in 1252, 1253 and 1255. During the 1700s it was an important centre for flax and hemp the raw materials required for rope manufacture much of which was used by the Royal Navy.

In 1791 two stage wagons a week stopped in the town on their journey to the capital 110 miles away. In the late 1700s the South Forty Foot Drain was cut providing access to the international port of Boston . The town's role as an important distribution centre continued with the railways in the 19th century and later as part of the main road system to the Midlands.

The market place was a thriving economic centre with horse fairs in May and October which continued until just after World War II. Weekly markets which were held for nearly 550 years ceased in the early 1800s, but restarted in 1882 continuing until their cessation in the late 1930s. To cater for the many traders and dealers there were approximately thirty-six hostelries in the town.

As vehicles became dominant Donington continued to service the transport system. It was a successful produce distribution centre for the Midlands with complementary services flourishing. With the advent of coach holidays from the Midlands to the Lincolnshire and Norfolk coasts the town also became a popular refreshment stop.

When the bypass was constructed in the 20th century passing traffic gradually dwindled and as a consequence Donington has become a quieter place.

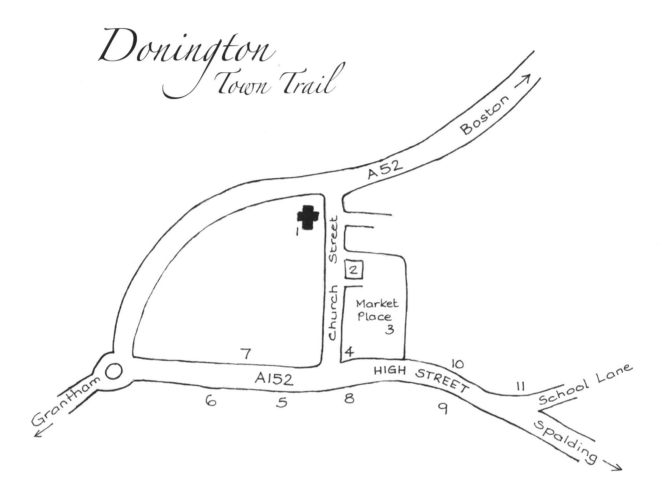

Donington
Town Trail

1. # Church of St Mary and Holy Rood *- Church Road*

Most of the church was built in the 14th century in the Perpendicular style, with traces of Norman (1100) and early English (1200) masonry. The window above the altar is 15th century, the stained glass being added in 1884. The mosaic reredos is Victorian. The nave is eighty-one feet long and twenty-two feet wide and the tower 140 feet high. It has eight bells with the earliest dating back to 1743.

In the north aisle is a stained glass memorial window to Banks, Flinders and Bass which was unveiled in 1980. The funds for this tribute were raised through donations and included contributions from the Commonwealth of Australia and Australian States. This, together with photographs and memorabilia, provides a dedicated area within the church to Donington's most famous resident Matthew Flinders. The 19th century memorial on the chancel wall to Matthew and other members of his family was requested by Flinders in his Will.

In the churchyard there are headstones on the graves of Matthew's father, sister, brother Samuel who sailed with Matthew to Australia, and his grandmother and grandfather. Matthew Flinders was buried in St James's Chapel, Hampstead Road, London, but his tombstone was removed during the building of Euston Station and the exact location is not known.

2. # Dress Shop *- Church Road*

This office was built by Ben Smith of Horbling in the 1700s. He was gravely concerned about the implications of the French Revolution and fearing an invasion he designed the building like a fortress. It has particularly thick walls giving it a very sturdy appearance. The building was built as office space for solicitors and it continued to service that profession until 2008. In 2011 it was converted into a ladies clothing shop.

Old Offices

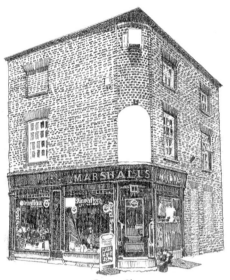

Corner Shop

3. *Market Place*

The general aspect of the market place has changed little since the 1700s although the noise and excitement of the many markets held there during Matthew's youth have ceased. Between 1740 and the early 1800s there were special markets where hemp and flax were sold. Stage coaches to various destinations including London stopped here, and it is likely Flinders would have used this transport.

As you look round the market place there are two prominent corner buildings. One has maintained its original proportions whereas the other has had the upper floor removed.

The unveiling of the Matthew Flinders statue by two of Captain Flinders great, great, great granddaughters Martha and Rachel Flinders-Lewis in the presence of an Australian Naval Officer took place in 2006. The figure is life size and at Matthew's feet is a representation of the cat that accompanied him on his voyages between 1799 - 1804. Matthew wrote in affectionate terms about his companion and in this extract he describes Trim's table manners:

'Trim was admitted upon the table of almost every officer and man in the ship. His modest reserve was such that his voice was not heard until everybody else was served. By a gently caressing mew, he petitioned for a little, little bit, a kind of tithe from the plate of each, and it was no purpose to refuse it, for Trim was enterprising in time of need as he was gentle and well bred in ordinary times. Without the greatest attention to each morsel in the person whom he had petitioned in vain, he would whip it off the fork with his paw, on its passage to the mouth with such dexterity and an air so graceful, that it rather excited admiration than envy'.

Trim

4. *Flinders House* – *Station Road*

Matthew was born in a house overlooking the market square. His father was a doctor and had a surgery attached to the dwelling. In the 1770s Matthew's father had to deal with many cases of Typhoid. A note in the burial register of 1772 said 'a great mortality had visited Donington'. The house and surgery survived until the early 1900s when it was demolished, but the present building has a plaque marking Matthew Flinders birthplace.

5. *Holmfield House* – *Station Road*

Matthew's neighbour was the Dods family. They resided in the town for nearly 200 years becoming wealthy coal and corn merchants well known in London's Coal Exchange. They also owned land and ran a number of businesses in Donington. At one time they employed nearly a hundred people.

The family's reign in the town came to an end during World War II when the last heir, Harold Dods of the Scots Guards, was killed on 18th June 1944. A German flying bomb crashed into the Guards Chapel in London where he was attending the morning service.

Holmfield House

The house was built in 1792 and is a typical Georgian building. It was constructed with local red bricks and is three bays wide and three storeys high. The house with its unusual moustache lintels above the windows was, with the exception of the church, the largest building in the town.

6. *Thatched Building* – *Station Road*

The building is mud and stud dating back to the 1600s and it was the office from which the Dods's family organised transportation of coal and corn by boat to the port at Boston. In the early 1800s they built a wharf where the Bridge End Causeway crossed over the Forty-Foot drain and expanded their transport business to include such diverse produce as animal feed, manure, stone, wine and spirits. Sadly the building is badly neglected and in need of renovation.

Dods's Office

7. The Black Bull - Market Place

The town had many taverns, beer houses and pubs that catered for people attending the frequent markets and travellers who stopped for rest and refreshment. Dating back to circa 1560 and refronted in the 18th century the Black Bull was a coaching inn providing stabling and accommodation. The exterior has changed little over the centuries and the interior has retained its old world charm.

The name 'Bull' usually signifies that the sport of Bull Baiting took place nearby. The bull would be tethered to a ring and set upon by dogs. This activity was banned in 1835.

8. The Peacock - High Street

This was one of the principal inns of the town during the 1700s and would have been familiar to Matthew. At its busiest it would have four rooms full of customers and sell between 400 - 600 pints during Friday and Saturday night. The twice yearly horse fairs spilled out of the market place into the High Street extending beyond The Peacock. As the markets ceased and the number of passing motorists declined the inn had to close in 1990 and it is now a private home with a plaque recording its former role.

9. The Red Cow - High Street

This inn was built in the early 1600s and bought by Thomas Cowley in 1680. He established a Thomas Cowley Trust and it took over the management of the hotel. In 1752 the inn was rebuilt at a cost of £390. It was considered the most prestigious coaching inn in Donington. At the rear of the premises there are many outbuildings, some were used as stabling and others as small businesses. Ropes were dried here and then transported to London.

The trustees sold the hotel in 1950 to Holes Brewery in Newark. It is a Grade II listed building now in need of renovation.

Pedlars

Thomas Cowley School

10. *Thomas Cowley School - High Street*

Thomas Cowley, born in 1625, was a rich London wool merchant who retired to Donington in 1680. He built Wykes Manor House two miles east of the village. He owned 734 acres, the Red Cow Hotel, a blacksmith's shop, a market garden, several houses and also received the income from the Manor of Wykes. These provided an annual income of £1,500. He died a bachelor in 1721 aged ninety six.

Cowley built and endowed the Free School in 1719. Matthew Flinders was a pupil being particularly good at mathematics and trigonometry. This particular skill was improved at the Horbling Grammar School by Revd John Shinglar. In his chosen career this talent proved extremely important.

The Cowley school was rebuilt in 1826 when it had 300 scholars, forty so poor they were clothed by charitable donations. The school has expanded over the years but maintains its link with the past by naming two of its houses after Flinders and his friend a fellow Lincolnshire explorer George Bass. In addition one of the school halls is named after Flinders.

Hay Field

George Bass

1771-1803

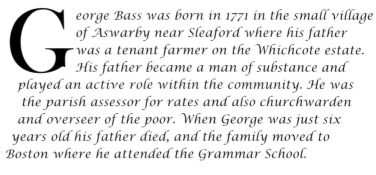

George Bass was born in 1771 in the small village of Aswarby near Sleaford where his father was a tenant farmer on the Whichcote estate. His father became a man of substance and played an active role within the community. He was the parish assessor for rates and also churchwarden and overseer of the poor. When George was just six years old his father died, and the family moved to Boston where he attended the Grammar School.

He was fascinated by the thought of a seafaring life, fuelled by seeing ships coming and going from the Haven in front of his home. His mother however was opposed to the idea and apprenticed him to a surgeon apothecary in the town. He became a member of the Company of Surgeons following an examination before the Court of Examiners on the 2nd April 1789 when he was eighteen years old. On the 1st July the following year, the same body approved his qualification as Surgeon 2nd Rate. He joined the Navy as a Surgeon's Mate shortly after receiving his qualification, but it took five years of service before his desire for adventure was granted. He joined HMS Reliance in April 1794 and sailed with his friend Matthew Flinders to New South Wales.

George was a resourceful man. He bought and stored on board a small, eight feet long dinghy named Tom Thumb. Following arrival at Port Jackson (now Sydney) Governor John Hunter allowed Bass and Flinders to explore uncharted waters on the east coast. In October 1795 they set sail in Tom Thumb and spent nine days in the area of Botany Bay and George River. In his journal Matthew Flinders describes how he, Bass and his servant Martin coped during a storm:

'Mr Bass kept the sheet of the sail in his hand... a single wrong movement, or a moments inattention, would have sent us to the bottom. The task of the boy was to bale out the water which, in spite of every care, the sea threw at us.'

On their return Governor Hunter was so impressed with their account of the region he founded a new township and named it Bankstown.

Exploration was interrupted in 1796 when Hunter sent HMS Reliance to Cape Town to obtain supplies and livestock. Unfortunately the expedition encountered terrible storms on the return journey. They lost most of the cargo and the ship was seriously damaged.

On 3rd December 1797 Bass was given another opportunity to explore. He and six volunteers set sail in a twenty-eight foot whaleboat. They had instructions from Governor Hunter to investigate the probability of a passage between the mainland and Van Diemen's Land (now Tasmania). The party had provisions for six weeks but the resourceful Bass extended that to eleven. He increased their food supply by catching fish and shooting birds and small animals. They sailed to Twofold Bay (later an important whaling centre), then Jarvis Bay (a future naval base) and Wilson's Point the

Tom Thumb in a storm.
Matthew Flinders, George Bass and his servant Martin

southernmost extremity of mainland Australia. He continued round the southern coast and became the first man to explore the coast of what is now Victoria.

They were unable to find conclusive evidence that Van Diemen's Land was an island, but the tides and curvature of the land suggested a strait or deep bay. There was also a constant heavy easterly swell and they experienced a strong tidal current consistent with a surge of water constricted by two bodies of land. On his return Hunter rewarded Bass for his ingenuity by granting him 100 acres of government land in Bankstown.

Following his adventures in the whaleboat there were short periods of exploration interspersed with duties on HMS Reliance. These included the transportation of personnel and convicts to various parts of New South Wales, and voyages to bring essential supplies to the burgeoning townships. However in 1798 Hunter decided another expedition to Van Diemen's Land was necessary.

In October he put Flinders in command of the sloop HMS Norfolk with orders to establish whether or not Van Diemen's Land was an island. This supposition made by Cook in 1770 was supported by conditions recorded by Bass during his earlier visit, and was believed by Hunter. Flinders accompanied by Bass and a volunteer crew of eight successfully found the passage. They then spent three months making a complete circuit of an island which had been regarded as an appendage of the mainland. In May 1799 while Bass was in Sydney he wrote to Sir Joseph explaining the discovery of the Strait:

'I discovered in latitude 39 degrees a strait which divided Van Diemen's Land from New South Wales. Governor Hunter being desirous that the Strait I had discovered should be further explored and surveyed found a volunteer in Lieut. M. Flinders of the Reliance. A sloop of twenty tons burthen was fitted for the purpose. We passed through the Strait and returned by the South Cape of New Holland.'

Flinders wrote of the journey:

'To the strait which had been the great object of research and whose discovery was now completed, Governor Hunter gave at my recommendation the name of Bass Strait … a just tribute to my friend.'

The passage between Van Deimen's Land and the mainland was an important discovery as it provided a route to the Indian Ocean which reduced the journey back to England by seven days.

Unfortunately Bass's exploits in the new continent had seriously undermined his health and he was discharged from the Navy. However his adventures on HMS Reliance were to influence the remaining years of his life. He purchased the brig Venus and planned to return to the continent as a merchant to provide supplies for the colony. Unfortunately by the time he returned to New South Wales others had recognised the commercial opportunities and the market was flooded with European goods. His cargo was put into store and he immediately embarked on a voyage to obtain meat from Tahiti, a commodity that was in very short supply. This expedition was concluded successfully and provided the means to plan another voyage.

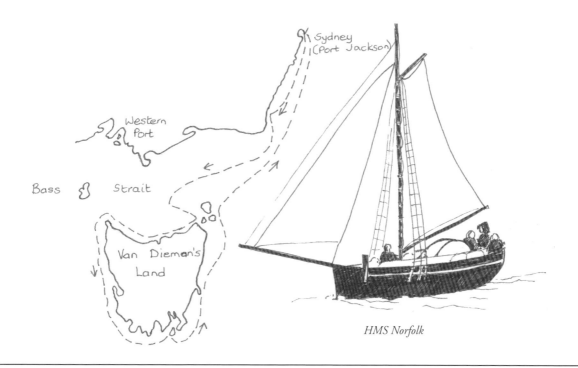

HMS Norfolk

His second venture was an ambitious one. He proposed to undertake fishing and sealing near New Zealand taking the salted meat and fish to Australia. He would then sail to England with seal pelts where they would be sold. The profit from these transactions would enable him to repair and restock the ship after which he would sail across the Pacific to South America to acquire farm animals. These would be transported live to New South Wales for the purpose of breeding.

Bass sailed from Port Jackson on the Venus on 5th February 1803. What happened thereafter is a mystery. Bass and his crew disappeared and were never seen again. Although many rumours circulated at the time there has been no satisfactory explanation for the disappearance of thirty-two year old Bass, his ship and his crew.

George Bass was an extraordinary man whose adventurous spirit suited the era into which he was born. Australia acknowledges his discoveries and his name lives on through Bass Straits, Point Bass, Bass Isles, Bass River and Bass Town.

Joseph Banks Country
Aswarby

Village House

This visit offers an opportunity to walk round an area that time seems to have forgotten. Modern bungalows are nowhere to be seen and the scattered homes of residents melt into the landscape. The village is so small a map is not required.

Aswarby is a collection of houses situated in parkland of the Whichcote's estate. The ambience is overwhelmingly peaceful being located in grazed meadows and mature trees. During the 19th century the grey stone workshops were converted to farm cottages and new brick farmhouses and a rectory were erected.

The village forms part of Aswarby Estate and it is managed by tenant farmers. In the centre of the village is the church of St Denis with scattered farms on the outskirts. One such residency is Grange Farm where George Bass was born and lived during his early childhood. His original home was demolished and replaced by a large farmhouse in the Victorian period.

The village was once famous for having a spring on the boundary with Osbournby reputed to have healing powers. However during the reign of Elizabeth I it was claimed a cow had drowned in the trough polluting the water. Gradually the healing powers were forgotten until a schoolmaster rediscovered the legend in 1731. Sir Francis Whichcote tried the water and reaffirmed the spring's former reputation. Believing the claims, vast crowds arrived hoping to improve their health. The Tally Ho hostelry was established to cater for their needs.

Celandine

Church of St Denis

The building dates back to the Norman period as testified by the magnificent south door and large font. It is a particularly grand edifice considering the small population.

George Bass was christened here in February 1771 and there is a memorial to him in the church near the south wall. His father was a prosperous farmer living most of his life in the village. He died when George was only six and his table tomb lies in the graveyard close to the south wall of the chancel.

Whichcote Crest

The boxed pews of 1847 were installed to combat the cold draughts in winter. The Whichcote crest is on the pulpit, Manorial pew and the stained glass windows in the nave. The painted boards on the tower walls were originally above the principal doorway of Aswarby Park. They were a notice to visitors that a family member had recently died. The burial vault lies below the raised platform with 17th century railings.

There are excellent leaflets in the church providing detailed information about the building and village.

JOSEPH BANKS COUNTRY
Sleaford

In the Roman period the main industry of the town was the mining of limestone from local stone quarries. It was a popular building material. Pub signs were once made of stone and at the Bull and Dog there is one dated 1689 and another at the White Hart dated 1691. The Domesday Book (1086) records the importance of mills in the town. There were eleven watermills on the river Slea in the Manor of Sleaford with another seven between Sleaford and Ruskington. Nationally this cluster was considered particularly valuable and unusually large. After 1070 Sleaford became part of extensive estates belonging to the Bishop of Lincoln. The Carre family acquired the land and Manor of Sleaford in 1559. They had a considerable impact on the town and donated a school, hospital and almshouses.

In the early 18th century rope making was an important industry. Hemp and flax were soaked to soften the fibres and then beaten using water powered hammers housed in Dam Mill. The fibres were finally twisted together along a stretch of land near the River Slea then known as the Rope Walk but now called Electric Station Road.

In the 1790s the town benefited from three new services: Turnpike Roads provided links with Peterborough and Tattershall, the latter supported by Sir Joseph Banks. He was also actively involved in the establishment of a canal further improving the transport infrastructure. Other supporters of the Sleaford Navigation were the influential family Anthony Taylor Peacock grandfather of the great entrepreneur Cecil Rhodes, and Benjamin Handley a solicitor and friend of Banks. In 1792 the Peacock family also co-founded the town's first bank Peacock Handley and Kirton.

Following completion of the canal in 1794 a variety of industries grew up along the wharf and the town prospered. Once the Slea became navigable to the river Witham it opened up cheap and easy transport to Boston and Lincoln, and this in turn provided access to the Trent and the Midlands. Transport and ancillary services became a major source of employment in the late 1700s and fuelled the general prosperity of the town.

From the mid-1700s to late 1800s there was a programme of regeneration and modernisation. In 1829 - 31 the whole town was flagged and drained, and in 1839 gas street lighting appeared. New buildings were mainly constructed of Ancaster stone and the impressive redevelopment earned the town the soubriquet Flower of Lincolnshire.

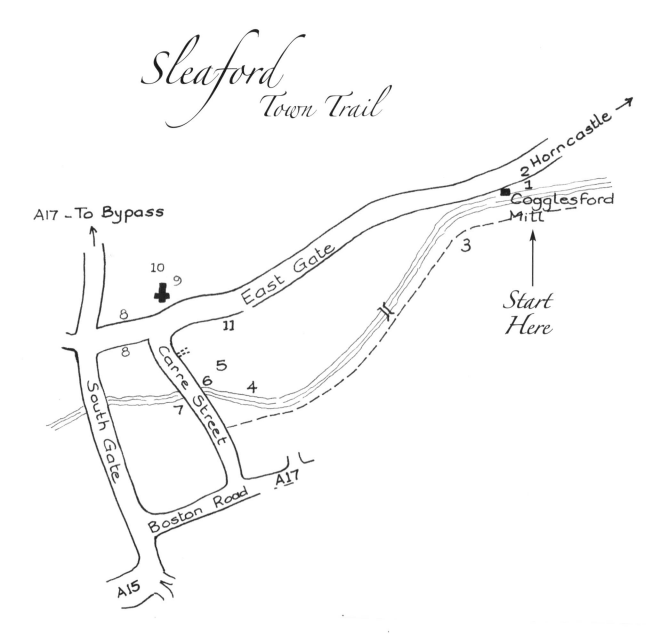

Sleaford
Town Trail

A17 — To Bypass

Horncastle

2

1 Cogglesford Mill

3

Start Here

East Gate

10
9
8
11
8
Carre Street
5
6
4
7
South Gate
A17
Boston Road
A15

1. # Cogglesford Mill

In a survey by William Hare in 1783 he records:

'The water mill called Coggleford Mill being a very good mill with two water wheels, four pairs of stones and all proper conveniences, also a good dwelling house and granary, a good stable with a granary over it and a small new granary built by the tenant; all brick and tiled except the stable, which is thatched.'

Cogglesford Mill

In 1793 the mill owner, William Almond, wrote to Joseph Banks supporting the proposed navigation and requesting a reservoir be formed near the Mill at the same time. This provided sufficient space for boats to manoeuvre and return following the route by which they arrived. That reservoir is the mill pond that exists today. It proved a wise decision as the ease of access helped his business to expand. This in turn enabled him to invest in the initial flotation of Navigation Company shares and he took an active role on the Committee of Proprietors after 1804.

2. # Mill House

It is a substantial building and provided spacious and comfortable accommodation. The conversion of the mill house in 2005 retained the original internal proportions of the building. This allows visitors to the restaurant to see the layout much as it would have been when the millers' families resided in the house.

3. *River Slea*

Follow the towpath on the south side of the river towards the town.

There had been earlier attempts to promote a canal but in 1791 a successful bid was finally made when Sir Joseph became directly involved. He accompanied William Jessop Surveyor, and Anthony Peacock the Navigation Company Chairman, when they took a boat trip to ascertain the river's suitability for development. Farmers who were concerned about the possible effect on the water level and irrigation had raised objections during previous attempts. Banks overcome these by suggesting the canal be developed along the Mill Stream rather than the Old River. When the canal was finally built it was thirteen and a half miles long and four to five feet deep. It had a drop of forty one feet six inches and to be functional it required seven locks and eight brick bridges. The estimated cost was £10,000.

The navigation was completed and opened for business in 1794. The cost to investors was approximately £15,000 considerably more than the submitted estimate. This became a busy waterway enabling large cargoes to be transported quickly and conveniently. It greatly increased the amount of grain coming into the town and the number of mills along the river increased. Manufacturers from outside the county also took advantage of the convenient transport system and commodities such as coal for the town's new gasworks eventually equalled grain in importance.

4. *Quayside*

The Hub started life as a warehouse but it now provides a large gallery space for modern arts and crafts and includes a cinema suite, cafe and craft shops. Originally the quay was part of the garden attached to the Almshouses. It was sold to the Navigation Company for £400 and provided space for the wharf, basin and warehouses. Packet Boats regularly left the wharf carrying passengers to Boston and Lincoln and in 1826 there was a weekly service to Nottingham and Derby. Following the advent of the railway in 1857 the Navigation began to decline finally closing in June 1878 after eighty four years of service.

Carre Street

5. Navigation House and Weighing House – off Carre Street

Navigation House was built in 1838 as the Navigation Company offices. It is reputed to be the sole surviving example of this type of building on the canals of Britain. Sir Joseph was asked to design the Company Seal when the Navigation was first established. A replica of that Seal was carved in stone and placed above the door of the offices. The emblems include a stook of corn and labourers depicted with corn and coal together with the motto 'the burden which is well borne becomes light'.

Navigation House

Collecting tolls became increasingly difficult as traffic increased. The amount charged depended on weight and the method used to calculate this was cumbersome. To overcome the problem it was decided that a weighing machine should be purchased and a 'Shed and Counting House' erected. The contract to build this very early example of Cotswold design was awarded to John Brotheway of Grantham. The building was opened in June 1838 at a cost of £191 12s. 9d. The weighing machine cost a further £69 9s. od.

Wharf Entrance

6. Wharf Entrance – Carre Street

It is not known how the gateway came to be at this location. One theory is that the arch was moved to this site in 1830 when Carre Street was built. It is assumed the arch originally gave access to what became a varied industrial centre on the main wharf. It once contained a number of industries including a steam mill, soda water factory, coach works, iron foundry, brick works, builders and breweries.

7. Money's Mill - off Carre Street

Money's Yard and mill are opposite the Wharf entrance. The mill was built by Henry Sutton, miller and baker of Sleaford at the time of the canal and it stood at its terminus. It is seventy feet high, has eight storeys and had three pairs of millstones.

The following is a description of Sleaford written in the early 19th century:

'Sleaford is an improving place, but especially within the last five or six years, during which period several enclosures have taken place; the river has been rendered navigable, and a turnpike road made over fens before impassable. From the navigation the inhabitants derive a considerable trade, and by road a direct communication is opened between the north-east quarter of the country and the metropolis, through the town.'

Moneys Mill

8. Market Place and Eastgate

Market Place Scene

The Angel Inn is now the Bristol Arcade which is a Grade II listed building. During Sir Joseph's life it catered for travellers and the coaching trade. Stage coaches came through the town daily from London to Hull stopping for fresh horses and delivering mail.

The Angel was also the scene of the inaugural meeting of the Sleaford Navigation on 29th December 1791. It was at this meeting the scheme put forward by the surveyor Mr. Jessop was formally adopted.

Following Royal Assent on the 11th June 1792 a celebration was organised. It took place on 22nd June when the Market Place became the scene of much merriment. Games, dancing, fireworks and 4,200 pints of beer were provided for the townspeople, while a celebration dinner was organised for the gentlemen of Sleaford and District.

9. *Church of St Denys* – *Market Place*

The origin of the present building is attributed to Bishop Alexander of Lincoln and is 12th century. The tower holds eight bells which were hung in 1796. The communion rails came from Lincoln Cathedral in the early 1770s. It was partially rebuilt and restored in the Victorian period following a lightning strike. William Turner painted the church which has an early broach spire. More details are available from guide books in the church.

Vicarage

10. *Vicarage* – *Market Place*

This delightful timber and brick house is a Grade II listed building and was built in the 1500s. It is the oldest surviving building in the town. The moulded stone gateway on the left has a rebuilt segmented arch and small brick coping. It is surmounted with a cross and piece of medieval masonry. The two storey red brick wing is an addition built in 1861. Inside there is a chimneypiece dated 1568.

Almshouses

11. *Almshouses* – *Eastgate*

Originally this was the site of the Carre Hospital and almshouses donated to the town in 1636. They were described as neat stone buildings and provided homes for twelve poor men with a woman or manservant to attend them. It previously covered a greater area but a portion was sold to the Sleaford Navigation to establish the wharf. Robert Carre endowed the hospital with tithes from Metheringham and Kirkby La Thorpe. It is believed these were demolished and new almshouses erected on the east side in the 1790s. The site was then redeveloped during the regeneration programme. The existing buildings were refronted in 1830 and additional almshouses and chapel were built in 1844. Further modernisation took place in the 20th century to provide updated accommodation for retired people. The chapel still exists but religious services have ceased.

Lincoln Imp

JOSEPH BANKS COUNTRY
Lincoln

Newport Arch

Lincoln is one of England's smaller cities. It is dominated by its magnificent Cathedral which sits as if enthroned on a prominence above the town. Houses and shops spill down the hill to the main thoroughfare and river below. Uphill Lincoln first established as a roman colonia became the administrative hub of the region and retains a wealth of beautiful old buildings. Downhill Lincoln with its river and marina provides an attractive area with facilities for commercial activity and the university.

Lincoln has seen phases of prosperity and decline throughout its history, but it was during the 12th century that it really thrived due mainly to the wool and textile trade. By mid century the city was amongst the wealthiest in England and Henry II bestowed one of many charters in 1157. The waterway system was at the heart of Lincoln's international trade with the Fossdyke canal providing a link to inland centres via the Trent and to Boston via the River Witham. The city was highly influential and ranked with Cambridge and York in importance.

The early system of transport was further improved in the 1700s when a network of navigable waterways was developed across the county. Sir Joseph successfully persuaded a reluctant City Council to improve the access for boats to the Brayford. As a result of this, together with the arrival of the railways and the industrial revolution, the population and prosperity of Lincoln grew rapidly.

Sir Joseph journeyed from London to Revesby each year during the autumn and he would always spend a few days in Lincoln. He attended the Lincoln Horse Races and was a patron of the very popular annual Stuff Ball at the Assembly Rooms.

This trail will take you round a part of uphill Lincoln that has changed little since Sir Joseph walked its pathways.

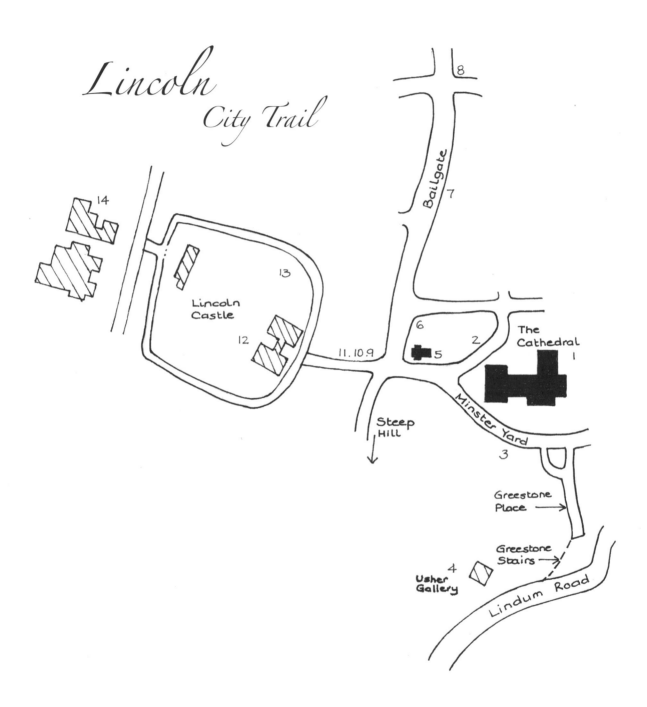

Lincoln
City Trail

1. Lincoln Cathedral

The original building commenced around 1072 and took twenty years to complete. After completion it suffered two disasters: in 1141 it was devastated by fire and then in 1185 an earthquake left much of the Cathedral in ruins. Very little of the Norman church survives although the central section of the West Front incorporates part of the original. The task of rebuilding commenced in 1192 under the direction of St Hugh of Lincoln and it is this building we enjoy today.

Inside on the south side of the great West Door is a tribute to Sir Joseph, with a quotation by Robert Hobart 1793: 'Wide as the world is, traces of you are to be found in every corner of it.' The plaque was unveiled by Australia's High Commissioner H. E. Philip Flood on 26th May 2000. Above the West Door there is a narrow walkway with a view of the nave known as 'Banks View'.

In a letter dated 19th September 1790 Dorothea Banks writes to a friend in Doncaster:

'We went to the Cathedral Sunday after the races, a sermon was preached for the benefit of the County Hospital by Mr. Thos. Monson. Lady Monson and Mrs. Neville stood at the church doors to collect for the charity.'

In the Seamen's Chapel in the North Transept are stained glass windows designed by Christopher Webb in 1953. The window on the right depicts Sir Joseph Banks at the top, beneath are George Bass and Matthew Flinders. The model ship to the right of the altar is of HMS Investigator, the ship Flinders sailed in during his circumnavigation of Australia. The Bell on the left is from HMS Tasman and is in memory of George Bass who discovered Bass Strait.

For more information there are excellent guide books in the shop.

2. Cathedral Close

In the 1300s The Close was surrounded by a twelve foot wall enclosing the properties of the Dean and Chapter. Walking round the Cathedral enclosure you will encounter parts of that wall and some of the arches that connected it to passageways and roads on the outside. The inhabitants formed an independent

Cathedral Close

community over which the City and Judicial authorities had no governing power. Opposite the West front of the Cathedral is a row of delightful houses built during the life of Sir Joseph. These are reputed to be the first homes in Lincoln to be given numbers.

The Precentory

3. Minster Yard

There is a wonderful grouping of houses, a sight that has hardly changed since the days Sir Joseph wandered through its precincts. While enjoying the architecture of past centuries take a moment to study The Precentory, a house with an attractive stone oriel window.

In September 1786 Sir Joseph, his wife and sister stayed for a week with Sir Richard Kaye Dean of Lincoln before continuing their journey to Revesby Abbey. In 1791 Sir Richard visited Sir Joseph's home at Spring Grove Middlesex for two days. As he was soon to take up residency in Southwell he offered Banks the use of his house in Lincoln during the annual Race Week. Richard Kaye was a friend who shared Banks enthusiasm for botanising and sponsored him at his election as Fellow of the Society of Antiquaries and the Royal Society.

4. Usher Gallery - Lindum Hill

Walk down Greestone Stairs in the Minster Yard to Lindum Hill. An excellent portrait of Joseph Banks, painted by Benjamin West, hangs on a stair wall in the reception area. It was executed shortly after his return from the Endeavour voyage and includes objects collected during the journey. Sir Joseph is wearing a Maori flax cloak and at his feet is a drawing by Sydney Parkinson, a young artist who accompanied him on the voyage.

Joseph was an imposing figure. He was six foot tall with dark hair and deep brown eyes. A rich handsome young man whose fascinating stories from strange new countries made him irresistible to London society.

5. St Mary Magdalen - Bailgate

Go through the Exchequer Gate arch and on the corner of Castle Square is a church originally built in 1290 but extensively rebuilt in 1882.

Greestone Stairs

6. White Hart Hotel - Bailgate

A hotel has stood on this site for many centuries. The impressive façade was built in the 1840s style and the present building has maintained many of its original features. Visitors are able to enjoy the ambience of times past. During Race Week Sir Joseph entertained guests and settled accounts here.

7. County Assembly Rooms - Bailgate

The Ball Room

Built in 1744 to provide a facility for community events. The exterior was altered in 1914 when a classical façade was added disguising its earlier origins. The building was the venue for the annual Grand Ball which was the finale of Race Week and regularly attended by Sir Joseph and Lady Dorothea.

On 8th September 1790 Dorothea wrote to a friend saying:

'We went to Lincoln for the Races, had a very agreeable meeting, more company than last year. Lord and Lady Monson, Mr. and Mrs. Fredk. Lumley, Robt. and Lady Theodosia Vyner, and several other families we are well acquainted with... There was good sport on the Race Ground one day, the other two but little.'

Sir Joseph regularly subscribed five guineas to the 'Ladies Plate' as did many of the County's gentry. It was also the venue for the annual Stuff Ball. The inaugural event took place in Alford on 12th October 1786 but later moved to Lincoln and continued until 1938. All those attending had to dress in a woollen garment. Lady Dorothea who was Patron of the Ball in 1789 recorded her comments in a letter dated 2nd October 1786:

'We are to go the 12th of this month to a ball, which is to be attended by most families in the county for the encouragement of the woollen manufacture, we are all to be dressed in a Stuff of the same colour. If we meet many of our acquaintance, think we may like it very well.'

Sir Joseph was Treasurer for the County Assembly rooms, resigning in September 1800. In 1790 the premises were broken into resulting in considerable damage. This included a painting which Banks had presented.

Castle Square

8. *Newport Arch - Bailgate*

This can be seen at the northern end of the Bailgate. It is the only Roman gateway in Britain that still has traffic regularly passing through it. Then, as now, the smaller arch formed part of a walkway for pedestrians.

9. *Timbered Building - Castle Square*

Built around 1543 it is believed to have been the residence of a wealthy merchant. Having a corner location it is an eye-catching building that provides an ideal base for the Tourist Information Centre. It was restored in 1929. When the plaster overlay was removed it revealed a sturdy timber framed building complementing the beautiful Georgian bow window.

10. *Georgian House - Castle Square*

Next to the Tourist Information Centre is a late 18th century house which includes a balustrade at roof level. This is an imposing building that adds greatly to the character of the square.

11. *Judges' Lodgings* - Castle Square

The Judges' Lodgings was designed by William Hayward and built in 1810. The design of this building was highly acclaimed in its day and still retains its original grandeur. Over the entrance is the Hanoverian Arms carved in stone. It is still used by judges when the Crown Courts are in session.

12. The Castle

The castle grounds cover an area of six acres. William the Conqueror ordered its building in 1068 and according to the Domesday Book 166 houses were demolished to provide the necessary land. The castle is surrounded by a high protective wall and, in the past, a moat. It was found that the moat did not retain water so Charles I decided to sell the land and it was used for building.

The castle housed the City's jail for many decades and some of those cells still exist. In addition there is a unique prison chapel with single boxed seats. These confine the convicts in a small wooden cell their only view being of the vicar in his pulpit. The Crown Court, built in the 1820s, is also situated in the grounds.

As High Sheriff of Lincolnshire Sir Joseph organised a meeting at the Lent Assizes on 11th March 1794. Those present agreed a five point plan for home defence in the event of a French invasion. They also agreed that the required troops and cavalry were to be paid for by 'gentlemen of weight and property'. To implement the home defence plan the Grand Jury proclaimed that local people should learn how to use arms and place themselves under the command of unpaid officers. This proved an unpopular decision and caused riots in some parts of Lincolnshire.

Lincoln Castle

Dorothea wrote later that year to her friend Miss Heber:

'I must begin my history with our first object when we set out on our travels, which were the Assizes at Lincoln. We were almost a week as a county meeting for the defence of the county kept us a little longer than the business of the Assizes would have detained us... My sister [she is referring to Sophia Sir Joseph's sister] and I, having curiosity to see what was going forward, went at different times into court for a short time and were amused with the High Sheriff's procession.'

13. Cob Hall

Situated within the grounds of the castle this round hall was added in the 13th century so that archers could defend the north and eastern side of the castle. In 1817 the County Gallows was transferred from the north west corner to the roof of Cobb Hall. The iron fittings can still be seen on the inside. The last public execution in 1849 was of two men aged twenty and twenty-four, who were convicted of murder.

14. Banks Conservatory – The Lawn

Leave the Castle by crossing the bridge behind the Court Rooms. The Lawn was built in the Victorian period as a hospital for the insane. It has undergone many changes since then and is now a public amenity centre.

Within the complex is the Banks Conservatory developed by the City Council as a tribute to Sir Joseph and his interest in botany. He regularly made arrangements for gardeners to travel on board both merchant and Royal Navy ships to collect seeds and cuttings and many were nurtured in the Botanic Gardens at Kew. The plants in the conservatory represent some of those collected by people sponsored by Banks.

Sir Joseph Banks Conservatory

Banksia Integrifolia

Lincolnshire Fen Birds

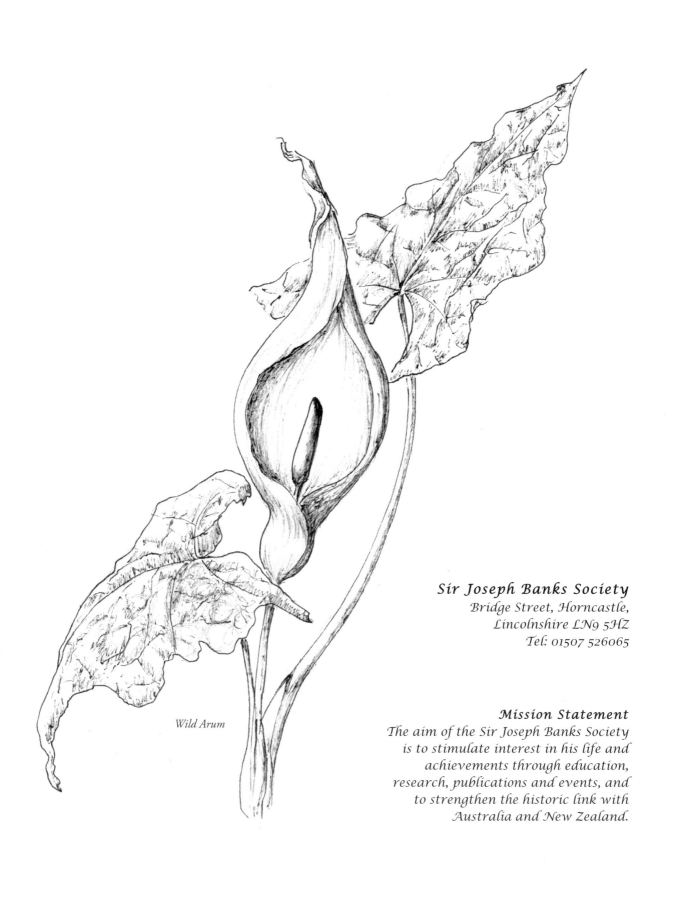

Wild Arum

Sir Joseph Banks Society
Bridge Street, Horncastle,
Lincolnshire LN9 5HZ
Tel: 01507 526065

Mission Statement
The aim of the Sir Joseph Banks Society
is to stimulate interest in his life and
achievements through education,
research, publications and events, and
to strengthen the historic link with
Australia and New Zealand.